THE 40 TOUGHEST SHOTS IN GOLF

THE 40 TOUGHEST SHOTS IN GOLF

A Pro's Guide to Better Shot Making and Lower Scoring

TODD SONES
with John Monteleone

Skyhorse Publishing

ACKNOWLEDGMENTS

Thank you to Ray and Jan Plote and their continued support of the Impact Golf School at Whitedeer Run Golf Club in Vernon Hills, Illinois, where the photographs for this book were taken. Thanks also to the photographers, Barry Havens and Mike Plunkett. I would like also to acknowledge and thank all the members of the PGA of America and members of the Top 100 Teachers in America as selected by *Golf Magazine*. This book is an accumulation of the many lessons I have learned from my peers.

Special thanks to writer John Monteleone, who not only collaborated with me to get my ideas down on paper but also suggested the idea of doing this book in the first place.

Skyhorse Publishing books may be purchased in bulk at special discounts for sales promotion, corporate gifts, fund-raising, or educational purposes. Special editions can also be created to specifications. For details, contact the Special Sales Department, Skyhorse Publishing, 307 West 36th Street, 11th Floor, New York, NY 10018 or info@skyhorsepublishing.com.

Skyhorse® and Skyhorse Publishing® are registered trademarks of Skyhorse Publishing, Inc.®, a Delaware corporation.

www.skyhorsepublishing.com

10 9 8 7 6 5 4 3 2 1

Library of Congress Cataloging-in-Publication Data is available on file.
ISBN: 978-1-61608-259-8

Printed in China

Contents

SECTION III Nothing Is Impossible

SECTION IV Down the Fairway

SECTION **V** **Pulling Rabbits Out of a Hat**

SECTION **VI** **On the Dance Floor**

Introduction

GOLF IS A GAME BEST PLAYED full of confidence and devoid of fear. If you've ever trudged into the woods or waded into a grass thicket to track down an errant ball—and who hasn't?—you know what I mean. Even the best players hit sloppy shots into tight spots or confront bad lies more frequently than you'd imagine. And for the average golfer, shots from remote, impossible-to-get-out-of places are much too often the norm. One mistake can sink a hole. A few blunders, and you've just scuttled the entire round.

The catch-22 is that, to master golf, you can't be afraid of hitting from tough lies (the rough) or difficult places (sand bunkers). You need to master your fear, and to do that, you need to prepare for the inevitable, next-to-impossible shots that can sidetrack even the best golfers. Only then can you beat the odds and reach that performance plateau so dear to hearts of golfers everywhere: Par.

My goal in *The 40 Toughest Shots in Golf* is to teach you the secrets of fearless golfing. Consider this a trip into the gladiator ring: here, you'll face 40 opponents. Each one is meaner and more dangerous than the next. Each one threatens to destroy your quest for par. But if you can defeat them, there won't be a shot in golf you won't be able to handle or any hole that you cannot par.

As a teacher, it amazes me how quickly students can improve their overall games and individual shots once they learn the correct techniques. Many of these shots are far easier than they look—all you need is the right guide and a little practice. As your expert advisor, I'll take responsibility for the technical stuff such as how to position your body and where to hold your club. All you need to do is follow directions and practice.

To keep things simple, I've cut the book into six sections. In the first section, "You

Hit It There, Now Play It," I'll explain how to hit a bevy of shots you'll encounter between the tee and the green: deep rough, hardpan, wood chips, and water. In "A Day at the Beach," I'll highlight the 11 most common sand bunker shots, from the fried egg to the long explosion shot, which many consider the hardest shot in the game.

Section three, "Nothing Is Impossible," is devoted to those situations when all seems lost: hitting through, under or over trees, swinging with little or no back-swing, taking opposite-hand shots, and hitting blind. In "Down the Fairway," you'll learn how to hit the fade, draw, knockdown into the wind, and how to make adjustments necessary to hit a ball below or above your feet, or balls that are on downhill or uphill lies.

Section five, "Pulling Rabbits Out of a Hat," shows you how to score when a sit-uation demands precise planning and execution. It includes instruction on how to hit a "Super Lob to a Tight Pin on an Elevated Green" and a "Chip from Heavy Rough Just off the Green." And section six, "On the Dance Floor," teaches you how to save strokes around the green. It's staggering how many shots players can save during a round with the putter, especially on days when the tee-to-green game isn't up to par. In all, you've got a compendium of how to hit 40 of golf's most difficult and/or demanding shots.

One way that you can use this book is to cherry-pick the shot or shots that trouble you the most. Read, then practice the techniques. Reread and practice some more. By returning to the text, you will pick up the nuances of each shot. This at-tention to detail and repetition will ingrain these techniques into your approach and you'll transform those "down and dirty" shots into the shining lights of your game.

This book is not filled with a lot of swing theory. It contains practical, step-by-step instruction on how to plan and hit golf's most troublesome shots. The instruc-tion is what I use with amateur students, so it is not so advanced that you must come to it with superior playing skills. It will help golfers of all skill levels. Of course, the better your swing is grounded in fundamentals, the better chance you'll have of quickly mastering these shots.

Learning the correct ways of hitting shots is the first—and most critical—step in improving your scores. You can become a better shot-maker. You can learn to enjoy the shots that frighten and challenge. Someday in the not-so-distant future, you'll actually enjoy playing them. And when fellow golfers ask you how you dropped so many strokes off your handicap, you can tell them about this book and point them in the direction of the nearest bookstore.

Now turn the page and begin.

SECTION

I

YOU

HIT IT

THERE,

NOW

PLAY IT

When the average golfer goes into the rough, too often he gets up to his ball and the first question he asks himself is, "What club do I need to reach the green?" That is putting the cart before the horse, in my book. Sure the distance is one factor, but the first thing to look at is your lie. It's no good fingering a wood when you have a sand wedge lie on your hands. The lie you have in most instances dictates the type of shot you have to hit.
—JOHNNY MILLER

Deep Rough

I AGREE WITH JOHNNY MILLER—it's a huge mistake if you don't first assess the lie of your ball. Examine and determine if grass is covering the ball. Look at how much grass is between the ball and the line of approach that the club shaft—especially the hosel—and clubface must take. Also check the direction the grass is growing. When it grows away from the target—the situation we're dealing with in this discussion—realize the grass will slow your clubhead and close the clubface. This happens because the hosel gets caught by the grass while the toe of the club keeps moving forward. The result is that the clubface twists and closes at impact.

USE MORE CLUB

When the ball is nestled in the rough and the grass is growing towards you, use one or two more clubs than usual. For instance, use a five-iron if you'd normally use a six- or seven-iron. For longer shots, unless you are unusually strong, you'll do better with a lofted fairway wood, such as a four-, five-, or seven-wood, than a long iron. In the rough, the sole of a fairway wood will part the grass and slide through easier than a midiron or long iron.

Aim the body left and assume a slightly open stance, ball positioned in the middle or just slightly forward of the midpoint of your body, and grip the club with a slightly open clubface.

TAKE AN ABRUPT SWING

Take a swing that is more upright than normal. Tighten your grip pressure and hit abruptly down into the ball. Hold the clubface open and make a steeper angle of approach than normal. This reduces the tendency to catch the grass too early in the forward swing. Keeping the clubface open, follow through with a full swing and finish.

Test the rough with a practice swing to determine how much resistance it will offer to your swing.

—BYRON NELSON

When in deep rough, grip the club with a slightly open clubface and make a steeper angle of approach than normal.

HITTING FROM THE CLOVER

Clover in the rough and on the fairways presents a special problem. When it gets between the clubface and the ball, it reduces backspin and often produces a "flyer." Flyers are shots that have reduced backspin, lower trajectory, and longer roll and carry. They are most likely to occur when the clover is high enough to get between the ball and clubface, but not so high as to reach to the top of the hosel. This holds true, as well, if water, including dew, rain, or liquid from plant material, reduces friction (which is necessary to promote backspin). Like a knuckleball or splitter in baseball, the ball will fly erratically.

Allow for the added distance you expect by swinging three-quarters or dropping down one club. You can also open the clubface and play a fade or cut.

SHOT BRIEFS ···· **DEEP ROUGH**

Common Mistakes
- Selecting the wrong club, that is, not matching the lie with the appropriate club; not using a club with enough loft
- In deeper grass, failing to open the clubface

Stance and Setup
- Take an open stance
- Open the clubface
- Position ball in middle or slightly forward of the middle of your stance

Pre-swing Thoughts
- Minimize club's contact with grass on backswing and downswing
- Imagine a left-to-right ball flight

Swing
- Take a steeper backswing than normal
- Tighten the grip pressure and hold the club open through impact

Many amateurs tend to lose their wits when they leave the fairway. It's as important to coolly pre-plan trouble shots as it is drives and approaches from closely-mown turf—more important, in fact, because of the risk of further compounding your original error.
—JACK NICKLAUS

Fluffy Rough

PICTURE A GOLF BALL SITTING ON 90 PERCENT AIR and 10 percent grass. If you ground your club behind this ball, you could dislodge it. And if that happens, the official rules of golf are clear—you "shall be deemed to have caused the ball to move. The penalty shall be one stroke. The ball shall be replaced unless the movement of the ball occurs after the player has begun his swing and he does not discontinue his swing."

WELCOME TO FLUFFY ROUGH

How you hit a ball in such a lie depends on your location and your immediate objective. If the green is in sight—maybe 165 yards away with a clear shot to the pin—you would combine some of the techniques used to hit shots from other troublesome lies, notably, shots from a fairway bunker (No. 8, see page 34) or from a flyer lie (No. 3, see page 9).

First, take a cautious approach—don't make the mistake of grounding your club behind the ball. Hover it at all times. This is a lie that you'll get at easier with a fairway or utility wood (a seven-wood, for example) than a long iron (two-, three-, or four-iron). So if you have a choice between hitting a 200-yard shot with a three-iron or a seven-wood, go with the wood.

When hitting shorter clubs from a fluffy lie in the rough, make sure you pick the ball cleanly off the top of the grass.

STAND ERECT

Stand more erect than usual and grip down an inch on the club. This will raise the bottom of the swing and encourage you to sweep the ball. Position the ball in the middle of the stance for short- and midirons or slightly forward of the midpoint if you're hitting a wood or long iron.

Prior to the swing, remind yourself to concentrate on tempo and keeping the clubhead moving level through impact. With shorter clubs, make a special effort not to swing under the ball with a deeply angled approach, but pick the ball cleanly off the top of the grass.

KEEP IT LOW

In the takeaway, keep the club low, finishing the backswing at the three-quarter position. Then swing down the target line. The ball should fly high unless you catch some grass between the

Watching the clubhead go back as you start your swing will probably ruin any chance you have of hitting a good shot. Anything you do wrong taking the clubhead back is not as bad as watching it. It is amazing how many golfers get into this habit.

—HARVEY PENICK

clubface and the ball, in which case it will behave like a flyer, that is, it will come out hot and roll more after landing.

Note: You can practice this shot by hitting balls teed from one-quarter to one-half inch. Observe the ball flight and catalog the distances you hit various irons with the sweeping swing. This will help you plan.

FLUFFY LIE NEAR GREEN

When you encounter a fluffy lie in the rough near the green, from 15 to 30 yards, you have more than one option. You can fly the ball to the pin and stop it or you can hit it low and run the ball to the pin. Here's how to hit each shot.

FLY IT

1. Position ball forward of the center of your stance and set hands slightly behind the ball.
2. Open stance and clubface.
3. Make a long swing without releasing the clubface.
4. After impact and during finish, keep left arm in chicken-wing position to promote holding off release of club.

RUN IT

1. Position ball in middle of stance and press hands forward to middle of front leg.
2. Square or slightly close clubface (to promote running after landing on green).
3. Make a short backswing and intercept ball along a shallow approach path.
4. Keep hands low on abbreviated follow through.

DRILL

Here is a simple drill to help you ingrain an important technique for hitting these greenside pitches from a fluffy lie: keeping your left wrist flat. Place a six-inch plastic ruler, a tongue depressor, or any flat stick under the back of the glove or under your watch band on your left hand. Position the stick or ruler so that it runs along the back of the hand up to the first set of knuckles. Practice swinging. This not only teaches you to keep the left wrist flat but also prevents the right hand from releasing prematurely and the clubhead from rolling over.

Common Mistakes
- Grounding the club at address, causing the ball to move from its original position (thus incurring a one-stroke penalty and the return of ball to original position)
- Making a descending approach to the ball

Stance and Setup
- Stand taller, grip down on club
- Play ball slightly forward of middle for longer irons and woods and in the middle for short irons
- Widen stance slightly

Pre-swing Thoughts
- Think tempo and solid contact
- Watch for possible flyer if there is a chance for grass to get between clubface and ball

Swing
- Low takeaway
- Take three-quarter backswing
- Sweep ball away, keeping approach shallower than normal

Grass (in the rough) growing toward the target offers less resistance, but the ball will tend to "fly" because grass between the ball and the clubface at impact diminishes backspin. Thus, you should take less club than normal and allow for plenty of run.
—JACK NICKLAUS

Flyer

THE KEY TO CORRECTLY APPROACHING A "FLYER LIE" SHOT is to focus on the word "flyer." With this lie, the ball is going to literally fly off the club, going much farther than usual. The obvious remedy? Take less club.

RECOGNITION IS THE KEY

The single most important factor in hitting this shot successfully is recognition: you must be able to detect a flyer lie. A flyer lie is any lie where the grass is certain to get between the club and the ball at impact. The ball is usually sitting up in the rough, with grass growing in the direction of the target. Flyer lies are most commonly found in the first cut of rough, where grass is high enough to come between the club and the ball but short enough to allow the ball to sit up. (Occasionally, they crop up in the fairway or in deeper rough.)

The number one mistake golfers make here is taking the same club they would for a normal lie. The common outcome is a shot that sails over the intended target or bounces and rolls farther than anticipated.

The second mistake occurs when golfers recognize the lie, but then alter their swings and hit the shot poorly. Commonly they'll try to "ease the throttle" in the downswing.

GRIP IT AND RIP IT

A flyer lie causes problems when hitting approach shots that require touch. But if there is enough distance between your ball and the pin to hit a fairway wood, by all means hit it. Fairway woods tend to be less affected by flyer lies because the club more easily slides through the grass. Even if the grass does catch the club slightly, the ball will jump off the clubhead and roll significantly. Your normal 210-yard, five-wood shots may travel 225 yards.

PLAYING THE FLYER LIE 100 YARDS IN

Playing a flyer lie from within 100 yards to the pin is extra tricky. Backspin is one of the keys to hitting perfect green shots. Without it, your ball will hit the green with no braking action, that is, backspin, and roll off the green. Because the ball flies with less backspin it goes farther and releases forward when it hits the green. Each of these factors makes it tough to control or predict the distance. Here is what I would do:

WHY DOES IT FLY?

The reason the ball travels a greater distance is because the blades of grass get trapped between the clubface and the ball. The grass creates a launching pad. There is just enough grass to get between the clubface and the ball, but not enough to create significant resistance to the club coming into the ball. This eliminates the spin and the ball knuckles or tumbles or otherwise erratically flies through the air. The lack of spin also makes it difficult to work the ball (fade or draw) or stop the ball on the green.

You can expect a five-iron shot to carry and roll at least 10 yards farther when hitting from a flyer lie. This means you should take one club less in this situation—a six-iron. Say, for example, you've got 170 yards to the pin and you would normally hit a six-iron. Pull out the seven-iron and take your normal swing. The ball may touch down a little short of your desired landing area, but your roll should make up for that.

Flyer lies are most commonly found in the first cut of rough.

First, I'd check out the 100 yards between my ball and the pin. If I have a clear path to the green that would enable me to hit a bump and run shot, I'd travel that path. To do so, I'd open my stance slightly and lean forward with the ball positioned in the center of my sternum. Then I'd choke down on the club for control, take a three-quarter backswing and finish low on my left side.

If I had a small amount of green to work with I'd choose another option: a soft fade or cut shot. Here's how to do it off a flyer:

1. Narrow your stance.
2. Open the face of your club slightly.
3. Position the ball just forward of normal (middle of stance).

You can tell a ball is a flyer because it's usually sitting up a little bit with some grass behind the ball. If the ball is sitting down, it's not going to fly as much, even if there is some grass behind it. If the grass is leaning toward your target, then the ball is really going to jump out of there. I take less club and I try to deaden the club through impact.

—STEVE STRICKER

4. Make a normal swing but feel as if you are holding the club off from releasing (toe rotating ahead of the heel) through impact. This technique will help to minimize the effect of the flyer lie and enable you to hit a high, soft shot to a tight pin.

SHOT BRIEFS FLYER

Common Mistakes
- Failure to recognize the flyer lie
- Take too much club
- Decelerate (fear of hitting the ball too far)

Stance and Setup
- Square stance slightly narrower than normal
- Grip down on club
- Play the ball in the center of your stance
  (or slightly forward of center for cut shot)
- Open clubface slightly

Pre-swing Thoughts
- Select less club
- Allow for roll when planning the distance of your shot

Swing
- Take three-quarter swing
- Focus on rhythm and tempo
- Finish with a complete follow-through

All sorts of things can go wrong when your ball is on hardpan because you can no longer slide the club underneath the ball. You can eliminate any type of flop shot or high shot. You have to hit the ball first, so play it back in your stance. A good word to think of is "pinch"—you want to pick the ball cleanly.
—BOB MURPHY

Hardpan

IF YOU EVER ATTEND A PGA TOUR GOLF TOURNAMENT, spend time at the practice tee. You'll see golfers working balls left to right, right to left, high, low, and when necessary, straight as an arrow. And yes, the balls will fly farther than you ever imagined. But note the sound each time a golfer makes contact—"Click." That is the sound of the clubface catching the ball pure—exactly how you want to hit a shot off hardpan.

Hitting off hardpan—a firm ground with little or no grass—separates professional golfers from those who only "swing the wrenches" on weekends. To most pros, a hardpan lie is not considered a trouble shot. In fact, finding their ball sitting on a firmer surface is sometimes even welcomed. It enables them to maximize the effect of precise ball striking and apply excellent spin and control.

But amateur golfers become anxious when faced with hardpan. If they don't hit the ball precisely, the club may bounce off the ground, resulting in a ball that is topped or hit fat. Golfers often overcompensate in this situation and try to strike the back of the ball. This leads to skulled shots—balls hit with the lead edge (lowest part of the clubface) in the center of the ball, which produces a low line drive and little control over the distance of the shot.

AVOID GROUNDING THE CLUB

The key to hitting a hardpan shot is to make sure the club does not bounce before hitting the ball. Grip down on the golf club and stand a little taller. Hang the
clubhead a little above the ball as you would when hitting a fairway bunker shot.
Play the ball toward the center of your stance but back about an inch to make sure
you strike the ball first.

Take a normal swing, but limit any excess body motion. In other words, don't
coil back as far as you usually would in an effort to quiet your lower body. Excess
body motion may give the club a chance to bounce. You want to strike the ball
cleanly. If you are concerned about generating power, grab an extra club and swing
smoothly.

Take a three-quarter backswing and concentrate on making a smooth transition
from the top of the backswing into the forward swing. Lead with your hands and
rotate into and through the hitting area. You'll hit the ball with the lower part of
the clubface so plan on a lower ball flight.

The key to hitting a ball resting on hardpan is to make sure the club does not bounce before striking the ball.

SKEPTICISM LEADS TO THE SKULLED SHOT

Playing a good shot off hardpan requires confidence. Maintain a positive approach and dismiss any negative thoughts. The fear of bouncing the club often leads a golfer to fall backward and lift the clubhead up as he swings through impact. When the body falls back and lifts up, the low point of your swing moves up also. The lead edge, rather than the clubface, makes contact with the ball and the result is a skulled shot.

To avoid this, make sure you swing through the shot. Keep your hands ahead of the club through impact. Try to maintain a smooth tempo, "pinch" the ball against the surface, and finish low. Shift your weight onto your front side in the finish.

One other tip for your short game. Don't grab a sand wedge out of your bag when faced with hitting off hardpan. More often than not, because of the increased degree of bounce needed for gliding through the sand, the sand wedge will bounce off the ground and the lead edge will blade (strike) the ball.

PITCH SHOT OFF HARDPAN

When faced with a pitch shot off hardpan, you're better off using a punch shot or bump-and-run. From this lie, either of those shots will offer better distance control and will also eliminate the possibility of bouncing the club and sending a screaming line drive across the green.

SHOT BRIEFS · · · · · · **HARDPAN** ·

Common Mistakes
- Using a club with too much bounce
- Grounding the club at address

Stance and Setup
- Stand taller
- Choke down an inch or two on the grip
- Play the ball an inch or two behind center (toward your rear foot)

Pre-swing Thoughts
- Don't ground the club
- Take an extra club and swing easy

Swing
- Take a three-quarter backswing
- Keep hands ahead of clubhead at impact
- Pinch the ball against the surface at impact

To play any golf shot correctly requires an unwavering concentration. The most perfect swing in the world needs direction, and plenty of it, and when its possessor begins to do a little mental daisy picking, something always goes wrong. A perfect attunement of every faculty is a thing even the finest players attain only very rarely, but by constantly keeping a vigilant watch over themselves they are able to shut out major vices over comparatively long period of time. Their concentration is not occasional, but extends to every single shot no matter how simple it may appear.
—BOBBY JONES

Off an Unstable Lie

GOLFING LEGEND BOBBY JONES MIGHT AS WELL have been talking directly to a golfer facing an unstable lie. You must concentrate even before you begin your pre-shot routine. There is the danger of losing a stroke by inadvertently causing the ball to move (see "Play Safe, Don't Touch" on page 20). My advice is "carelessness out, concentration in." Bobby Jones believed that the "powers of concentration alone could not make up for any vast deficiency of skill. . ." but concentration was an integral component of a good round, especially when facing a troublesome lie, such as a ball resting on pine needles, twigs, or other loose impediments.

PLAY IT LIKE A FAIRWAY BUNKER SHOT

This shot should be played like a shot from a fairway bunker: you need to avoid contact with unstable material and pick the ball cleanly off the lie. Your objective is to catch the golf ball first, ensuring solid contact. For example, when hitting off pine needles, if you hit the pine needles before the ball, the ball will move and will miss clean, crisp contact on the center of the club, thus creating a poor shot.

Select a club that is one or two clubs stronger than usual. Remember, when you "pick" a shot, you are not getting the use of the entire clubface. You are hitting the ball with lowest part of the club. Because you're contacting the ball on the lower part of the club your trajectory will lower. Your ball flight will be shorter and lower than normal, but the ball will typically release and roll farther than normal.

In your setup, center the ball in your stance. Your goal is to hit the ball first, using the front edge of the sole (bottom of the club) and lower portion of the clubface, much like you would in a fairway bunker when you pick the ball cleanly off the sand and displace very little. Keep your lower body quiet throughout the swing. Be

Hitting a ball on an unstable lie requires that you avoid contact with the unstable material and pick the ball cleanly.

careful not to bottom out your swing behind the ball, which you have to guard against when using a highly lofted club (pitching wedge, sand wedge, or lob wedge). Whenever possible, drop down to a lower lofted club, grip down on the club, square the clubface along the target line and hit crisply into the back of the ball, leaving a thin divot in front of the ball. Use a three-quarter takeaway and concentrate on making solid contact.

In playing from twigs, leaves, pine needles or similar loose materials, try to avoid grounding the club as you set up to the shot, thereby minimizing the risk of incurring a penalty for moving the ball. On full shots where the lie is clean, the ball will usually behave much as it does from the fairway, so swing normally.

—JACK NICKLAUS

PLAY SAFE, DON'T TOUCH

A ball lies in the rough on a patch of loose twigs. The player removes a twig that lies about six inches behind he ball. The ball does not move. However, a few seconds later, as the player is selecting a club, a gust of wind causes the ball to move. Does the player incur a penalty?

Yes, one stroke. The rules of golf are clear on this: "Through the green, if the ball moves before the player has addressed it but after any loose impediment lying within a club-length of it has been touched by the player, his partner or either of their caddies, the player shall be deemed to have caused the ball to move. *The penalty shall be one stroke.* The ball shall be replaced unless the movement of the ball occurs after the player has begun his swing and he does not discontinue his swing."

For the record, here are the definitions that apply with this rule.

Through the green: The whole area of the course except the teeing ground (starting place for the hole to be played) and putting green of the hole being played and all hazards on the course. A hazard is any bunker, sea, lake, pond, river, ditch, surface drainage ditch, or other de-fined water area; lateral water hazards are defined by red stakes or lines and regular water hazards are defined by yellow stakes or lines.

Addressing the ball: A player has "addressed the ball" when he has taken his stance (when a player has placed his feet in position in prepa-ration making a stroke) and has grounded his club, except that in a hazard a player has addressed the ball when he has taken his stance.

Loose impediment: Denotes natural objects not fixed or growing and not adhering to the ball, and includes stones not solidly embedded, leaves, twigs, branches and the like, dung, worms and insects, and casts or heaps made by them. Snow and ice are either casual water or loose impediments, at the option of the player. Sand and loose soil are loose impediments on the putting green, but not elsewhere on the course.

Common Mistakes
- Failure to select stronger club (drop down one or two clubs)
- Carelessness when addressing ball, causing it to move

Stance and Setup
- Align stance parallel to target line, square clubface
- Grip down on the club, stand taller and closer to the ball

Pre-swing Thoughts
- Allow for lower trajectory (bottom of club will contact ball)
- Hover club to avoid inadvertently causing ball to move while at address
- With highly lofted clubs, avoid bottom out swing before hitting ball (thus fluffing the shot)

Swing
- Keep lower body quiet
- Take club back three-quarters
- Pick ball cleanly, taking shallow divot

*The difference between a sand trap and water is the
difference between a car crash and an airplane crash.
You have a chance of recovering from a car crash.*
—BOBBY JONES

Water

ONE OF THE GREATEST MISTAKES IN GOLF is trying to hit a ball that is
not hittable. As this book shows, these instances are rarer than most golfers think.
But water shots are the exception. If your ball is in water, you probably have a
better chance of winning the Open than of getting a clean shot at it.

That is, unless less than half of the ball is submerged. If the ball is completely
submerged, forget it. Take the penalty stroke and hit from the drop area. But if one-
half or more of the ball is above the water line, I suggest you go for it. Here's how:

SELECT THE RIGHT "PADDLE"

The distance you're facing dictates club selection and which part of the clubhead
you'll use. For a longer shot—in this case, one that's 15 yards or more—you need to
knife through the water, much as you would slice through a wet sand bunker. Use
a nine-iron or eight-iron rather than a wedge. The nine-iron or eight-iron will displace enough water to carry the ball out of the water, not to mention carry the ball
farther than a wedge. If you're facing a shorter shot, use a wedge. Hit with the back-
side of the sole of the clubhead so it doesn't dig deeply into the water. You'll get less
carry but more height. (Oh, and in either case, plan on getting wet.)

STANCE AND SETUP

If you are faced with hitting a short greenside approach shot in which the stance requires one foot in the water, take off your shoe and sock. Open your stance, one foot in the water and one foot on dry land. Lean into the embankment. Aim left of the target. Position the ball in the mid-point of your stance. Set the clubface slightly open, and grip down on the club an inch or two.

If you are hitting a longer shot (more than 15 yards), make the following adjustments after taking the basic stance and setup: select the nine-iron or eight-iron, square or slightly close the clubface.

> *Only bullfighting and the water hole are left as vestigial evidence of what bloody savage man used to be. Only in golf is this sort of contrived swindle allowed.*
>
> **—TOMMY BOLT**

CASUAL WATER

Casual water is any water on a course that isn't part of a hazard. You are entitled to relief from it. Puddles left after rainstorms or thunderstorms, over-watered fairways or rough that leave standing water, or poorly drained low areas that collect water on the surface all qualify as casual water. You can take relief anytime water seeps over the edges of your shoe soles when standing at address. If you're not certain about whether you're entitled to relief here is a simple test. Take your stance and wiggle your feet, pressing down on the turf. If water seeps over your edges of your sole, you're in casual water.

Your nearest relief may take you out of casual water but leave you on soggy turf. You can make a good shot using the following adjustments:

1. Position the ball in the center of your stance.
2. Hover the club just behind the ball at address.
3. Concentrate on sweeping the ball, picking the ball cleanly off the turf.
4. Take extra club and keep your lower body quiet throughout the swing, much as you would when hitting a fairway bunker shot.

> *Being a Scotsman, I am naturally opposed to water in its undiluted state.*
>
> **—DR. ALISTER MACKENZIE**

PRE-SWING THOUGHTS

Think of the shot as an explosion shot from a sand bunker. Concentrate on a full swing and follow through—you must move to a full finish at the end of the swing.

SWING

Make an abrupt backswing, right elbow tucked with an early wrist cock. Drop the clubhead down hard behind the ball. Keep the clubhead moving through the impact area and beyond. Do not "stick the club" in the muck or water. Move it through, out and up. Make sure that you finish your swing on the left side (forward) of your body.

Careful evaluation is the key when hitting a ball in water. If one-half or more of the ball is above the water line, you can hit it.

Common Mistakes
- Failure to select the correct club: a nine-iron or eight-iron for distances of more than 15 yards, a wedge for shorter distances
- Trying to hit a ball that is more than one-half submerged

Stance and Setup
- Open your stance, position ball in the middle of your stance
- Hover the club over ball (and water)

Pre-swing Thoughts
- Think of exploding the ball from the hazard or in this case, if you will, splashing it
- Think positively: "I'm going to get wet but it's worth it to get my ball back in play. This could be the greatest recovery shot of my life."

Swing
- Make a steep takeaway
- Drop the club about an inch or two behind the ball
- Accelerate through impact and finish the swing

Golf is a game that evolved over humps, hollows, sand craters, ridges, dikes, and clumps of heather and gorse. These features made up a game that is a trial of luck and ingenuity. How dull to have no obstacles to dodge or need no "escape" shots in one's repertoire.
—PETER THOMSON

From a Divot

DIVOT LIES ARE AN UNAVOIDABLE PART OF GOLF, even for the best golfers. The most common mistake that players make with this shot is trying to hit with a high trajectory. For example, if you are 75 yards form the pin, a distance that would normally call for you to hit a sand wedge, but stuck in a divot, you aren't going to get a 75-yard loft. The ball will fly at a lower trajectory, because the clubface strikes the ball on its lower part, in effect de-lofting the clubface.

Some players try to add height to the ball flight by scooping the ball out of the divot. The results are disastrous—usually a fat shot or a skulled shot. These mis-hits either come up short or scoot low across and beyond the green.

Instead, plan for a lower flight and a little bit of roll out after your ball lands on the green. Take at least one or even two clubs more. At 75 yards, if you normally hit a sand wedge, take a pitching wedge or nine-iron.

Play the ball in the center of your stance. Align the clubface and your feet slightly open as you would in a long bunker shot. Narrow your stance slightly and stand closer. Grip down between one inch and one and one-half inches. Take the club back three-quarters, and keep your balance throughout the swing.

DROP THE CLUBHEAD
ON THE BACK OF THE BALL

You cannot come into this shot with a shallow angle. If you do, you won't catch the bottom of the ball. So approach the ball with a descending blow. Hinge the golf club on the takeaway and make sure that you hit the ball before hitting the ground on the downswing. Use the natural coiling and uncoiling of the body, holding onto the club firmly through impact, and uncoil as you swing through the shot to a full finish.

Allow for the ball to come out lower than normal with a slight left to right flight and a little roll after landing on the green.

PRACTICE

The practice range is an ideal place to find divots for practice shots. Hit from the front, back, and sides of the divots. The edges of divots will allow an iron to pass through to the ball. Hit from shallow and deep divots to get a feel for how you must adjust the downswing to catch the ball solidly.

You must accept your disappointments and triumphs equally.

—HARVEY PENICK

When hitting a ball from a divot plan for a shot that has lower flight and a little bit of roll after it lands on the green.

SANDED DIVOTS, SOGGY TURF, AND ROUGH

A ball in a sanded divot should be played as if you were hitting from a fairway bunker. When you are a considerable distance from the target, grip down, stand taller and concentrate on striking the ball first. When you are less than 90 yards, consider cutting across the ball with a club whose normal carry is 30% more than needed, such as hitting a nine-iron for the 90-yard shot.

When turf gets wet it gets heavy and more difficult to penetrate. Making contact with it prior to contacting the ball often results in a fat shot that falls well short of the target. When the turf is wet, concentrate on sweeping the ball with a minimal amount of contact with the ground. Try this technique:

1. Because this type of contact results in a lower ball flight (due to contact with the lowest part of the clubface), take an extra club to add back the required distance.

2. Position the ball in the center of your stance.

3. Grip down and hover the club just behind the ball at address.

4. Much as you would when hitting from a fairway bunker, keep your lower body quiet throughout the swing and try to make clean contact with the ball.

A ball in the rough can present a similar challenge. So if you find your ball nestled down in the rough, try the following techniques and you will successfully execute this shot.

1. Select a higher-lofted fairway wood, such as a five- or seven-wood. Distance is not the primary objective. Foremost among your objectives is successfully moving the ball out of the rough and down the fairway.

2. Grip down on the club, perhaps an inch or so. Aim left and open the clubface up to 20 degrees from square to the target line. Hover the clubhead behind and above the ball. Take a few practice swings to make sure the clubhead does not get tangled up in the blades of grass.

3. Reset your stance and position the ball in the center (even with your sternum) of your stance.

4. Maintain your balance throughout the swing. Swing under control.

Common Mistakes
- Trying to hit this shot with high trajectory
- Scooping ball instead of hitting down and through the ball

Stance and Setup
- Position ball in center of stance
- Stand closer and take a narrow, slightly open alignment and open clubface
- Grip down an inch or two

Pre-swing Thoughts
- Plan a shot that has a lower trajectory
- Select more club than distance calls for
- Allow for left-to-right flight and roll out after landing
- Think tempo and solid contact, not "hit"

Swing
- Hinge the club on the takeaway
- Swing down through the ball, keeping the clubface open
- Uncoil and rotate out of the shot to full finish

A

DAY

AT THE

BEACH

Bunkers are not placed on a course haphazard, but they are made at particular places to catch particular kinds of defective shots.
—JAMES BRAID

Fairway Sand Bunker

THE SAND BUNKER ON THE LEFT SIDE OF THE FAIRWAY of the 18th hole of Augusta National has caught many "defective" shots from the tee. None is more famous than the one-iron that Sandy Lyle landed there in the final round of the 1988 Masters.

Lyle, who was trying to become the first Briton to win the Masters, came to the 18th needing a par to stay tied for the lead with Mark Calcavecchia or a birdie to win the tournament outright. His ball was in the bunker 150 yards to an uphill green. The pin stood in the front left side of the green. The ball rested cleanly on a slight uphill slope.

Lyle dug in and anchored his body. He gripped down an inch on his seven-iron. Then he swung, nipping the ball perfectly and carrying it beyond the flag where it drew back to 12 feet of the pin. He sank the clutch putt and donned the coveted Masters green jacket for the first time.

Lyle recalls the momentous shot:

"The shot I faced was a very dangerous one. I was playing from a very steep-faced bunker, and I couldn't see the pin from where I was. There was a very real chance that I might catch the lip and have the ball end up in the bunker right in front of me, and that would have meant a double bogey or worse. The pin was on the front of the green, and there was a bunker short and left of it as well. There were so many things that might go wrong.

"The shot called for seven-iron, and I had to pick it cleanly or it would surely hit the lip. Under those circumstances, and with your body leaning away from the target, it is necessary to keep the lower body very still and swing mostly with your arms. You move the ball back in the stance a bit to make sure you hit it before you hit the sand. Dig the feet in solidly, and grip down a bit to shorten up the club to make sure you don't catch the sand before the ball.

"If all worked according to plan I thought I could get it somewhere on the green. I did, and I ended up 12 or so feet from the hole. It was a nice bonus to make the putt."

Sandy Lyle certainly played his most memorable fairway bunker shot by the book. Note that his first consideration was to select a club that would get his ball over the lip and safely out of the bunker. Failing to select the club that will provide the needed loft is one of the most common mistakes made. So when looking at the lip always allow more elevation than normal. You need first to get up and out. Distance is an important consideration, but it's not the primary one.

More often than not, you won't face a bunker lip as steep as the one on the 18th fairway at Augusta. Modern golf architects design most fairway sand bunkers with fairly low lips so that you can play toward the target. And most greenskeepers keep the sand in the fairway bunker relatively firm so that the ball sits up and is accessible to a well-executed stroke. Here's how to hit a fairway sand bunker shot:

GET OVER IT

Select a club that will get you safely over the lip between you and your target. If the lip is low enough to accommodate a stronger club, use it. For example, if you normally hit an eight-iron 150 yards, then hit the seven-iron or even a six-iron. However, remember you are contacting the ball with the bottom third of the club, thus using less than the full loft. The ball will fly lower than normal.

Dig in your feet slightly (don't go so deep that the sole edges are covered with sand). You don't want to lower yourself too much because this will lower the bottom of swing arc (which is catastrophic when trying to pick a ball cleanly). Put a little more pressure and digging on the inside of the back foot and forward press your back knee toward the target. Lift your chest and stand slightly taller, keeping your chin off your chest. Open the face of the club slightly (five to 10 degrees) and grip down on the club.

You're setting up to hit a slight cut or fade. It's easier to hit a slight cut shot because this shot minimizes the coiling and uncoiling—or loading and unloading—

Select a club that will get you safely over the lip between you and your target. If the lip is low enough to accommodate a stronger club and distance is needed, use it. When setting up *(#1)* to hit a fairway bunker shot dig in your feet slightly (don't go so deep that your sole edges are covered with sand). You're setting up to hit a slight cut or fade because this shot minimizes the coiling *(#2–#4)* and uncoiling *(#5–#10)*—or loading and unloading—of the body. Open the face of the club slightly (five to 10 degrees) and grip down on the club.

The key to hitting a fairway bunker shot is you have to stay really still on it. I try to think of getting the ball early (before the sand), and that gets the ball up quicker. I really focus on the exact spot on the ball I want to hit. If I'm close to the lip, I don't necessarily move the ball back in my stance.

—**FRANK NOBILO**

of the body. By contrast, a right-to-left shot requires a fuller loading action and thus represents a greater risk for moving the body and hitting the shot fat or skulling it. It is also easier to hit a slight fade because the open clubface slides through the sand. If the clubface were closed it would dig into the sand.

When faced with using either a long iron or a lofted fairway wood, choose the fairway wood. Because of the sole plate and mass of the clubhead, the fairway wood will slide a little in the sand and not dig in deeply. Properly maintained fairway bunkers, that is, those having firm sand, are receptive to fairway woods. And if there is no lip or little appreciable height to the lip you need not worry about elevation. The natural shallower arc of a fairway wood also enables you to make a

ESCAPING FROM A POT BUNKER

Links courses often feature pot bunkers, many of them in the fairway as well as alongside. Some are more than six feet tall. Escape is the operative word when faced with this shot. Align your feet slightly to the left of your target line. The leading edge of your open clubface should be to the right of the target line, while the shaft should be perpendicular to the target line.

In the backswing hinge the wrists swinging the club up with the right elbow tucked in, close to the body. Swing along your shoulder line and have the club enter the sand one to two inches behind the ball. Make a sharp, forceful descending downswing. Keep the club moving and allow a cushion of sand to pop the ball almost up and out.

SLIDE RULE

The legs are the foundation of the swing. When the lower body supports the motion of the upper body, a golfer is able to maintain balance. When the body is in balance, the golfer can swing at maximum speed and still make solid contact.

One reason golfers lose control of the lower body is they misunderstand how the weight shift should happen. When a player tries to shift his weight over the right (back) leg, he often slides the lower body away from the target. This leads to the upper body shifting toward the target to maintain balance. The result is a reverse weight shift—left on the backswing, right on the downswing—and a loss of power.

A proper weight shift is the result of the lower body supporting and somewhat resisting the upper body as it coils. During the takeaway, the shoulders, arms, and club should start the swing while the lower body stays passive. At a certain point, depending on the individual's flexibility, the hips will begin to turn and join the backswing.

A great way to improve your balance and train the lower body to form a solid base is to hit shots from a fairway bunker. Because of the lack of solid footing, the sand forces you to keep the lower body quiet to maintain balance. When most of your swings are making solid contact and you're finishing in balance, you have achieved a quiet lower body, which will help maximize power and consistency in your swing.

clean pass at the ball. Set the wood slightly open as well, and start the ball on a line that is slightly left of the target.

When hitting an iron, position the ball at the center of the stance. With a fairway wood, position the ball an inch to two inches forward of center.

Keep the legs and lower body relatively quiet during the swing. This doesn't mean totally "dead legs," with no flex. It means you should maintain total balance and consistent tempo and not add any extra "hit" in the downswing and through impact. Swing through to a balanced finish facing the target and on your forward leg.

FAIRWAY BUNKER SHOT

Common Mistakes
- Failing to select a club with enough loft to get your shot over the lip of the bunker between you and the target
- Overswing, losing balance in the swing, and mis-hitting the shot

Stance and Setup
- Dig in the feet, putting slightly more pressure on inside of back foot and forward pressing the back knee
- Stand taller, chin off the chest
- Set the clubface slightly open, aim left of the target and play for a slight cut or fade

Pre-swing Thoughts
- Think, "Pick it cleanly"
- Allow for loss of distance with cut or fade ball flight and grip down on club—take one or two extra clubs

Swing
- Stay balanced, make clean contact
- Keep lower body quiet
- Swing to a full finish

If you practice your bunker game and learn a few fundamentals, playing a ball out of a greenside bunker is not a difficult shot, even for the average golfer.
—HARVEY PENICK

Greenside Bunker Shot, Ball Sitting Up

YOU MIGHT THINK IT UNUSUAL THAT I'VE INCLUDED THE "garden variety" sand bunker shot as one of golf's toughest. But over my years of teaching, I've found that almost all shots from bunkers strike fear in the hearts of players. You've heard television's golf broadcasters comment that "he's got an easy bunker shot. His uphill lie will help him get the ball up and stop quickly." Even the venerable golfing legend Walter Hagen subscribed to the bunker shot's relative ease of execution when he remarked, "The bunker shot is the easiest shot in golf—you don't even have to hit the ball."

Yes, it's an easy shot if you understand how to execute it and you have the basic skills to pull it off. But many players never develop this skill, and allow bunkers to frighten them for their entire golfing lives. Here's how to step away from their ranks.

SAND WEDGE: GLIDES, SKIPS, OR BOUNCES

Some people think a sand wedge is for hitting golf balls. They are wrong. Consider the club for a minute: Its trailing edge is lower than the leading edge by a greater degree than the other irons in your bag. Typically, a set of irons will have one to three degrees of bounce (the curvature on the bottom or sole of a sand wedge, which helps prevent the club from digging too much into the sand and allows the clubhead to move easily through it). A sand iron, which has 10 to 16 degrees of bounce, is designed to glide through rather than dig into the sand. The sand wedge has more loft, normally from 54 to 57 degrees, as compared to the pitching wedge at 47 to 50 degrees. The sand wedge is heavier than any of the other irons. In short, it is designed to displace sand. And that's what you'll use it for: hit-

NECESSITY IS THE MOTHER OF INVENTION

Golfing legend Gene Sarazen invented the sand wedge during the winter months of 1931–32. In preparing for the 1932 British Open he searched for a way to meet the challenge of the multitude of bunkers of the Open Course at Prince's, Sandwich. At the time players escaped from greenside bunkers using a sharp-bladed nine-iron to cut a slice of sand from beneath the ball. It was a dicey shot that didn't always produce good results, a shot for which Sarazen was determined to find a better way.

One day while taking a flying lesson, Sarazen noticed that in order to make the tail portion of the plane rise, the elevator on the horizontal part of the tail needed to be turned downward. This positioned the trailing edge of the elevator lower than the leading edge. The elevator's resistance against the onrushing air forced the tail (and plane) up. Could the same principle work on a golf club so that the club wouldn't dig?

Sarazen set about finding out. He soldered his nine-iron so that when it entered the sand it glided under the ball and splashed it out In a spray of sand. He quietly practiced with it at the 1932 British Open, hiding the head of the club by placing it upside down in his bag and then taking it to his hotel room each evening. Sarazen's inspiration and practice paid immediate dividends. He won the tournament with a record score of 283, which stood until 1950 (when South African Bobby Locke won the Open with the first-ever sub-280 four-round total).

SAND BUNKERS VS. WASTE AREAS

Sand bunkers are hazards. Under the rules of golf you may not ground your club at address or hit the sand on your backswing. You can touch the sand only as part of your downswing. You cannot take a practice swing, rest your club in the sand while waiting to hit, or in any way test the texture of the sand. It's a one shot penalty if you do.

Waste areas are large sandy areas that appear to be bunkers. They often include clumps of wild grasses, thatches of brambles, and even rocks. You play them just as you would any other part of the golf courses. However, it's a good practice to treat them just like a bunker. This will reinforce your bunker-shot techniques and chances of getting out successfully.

ting the sand in front of your ball and literally throwing the sand and the ball into the air. It is the one shot in which you do not have to hit the ball.

FORWARD THINKING

The most common mistakes are positioning the ball too far back in the stance, and placing too much weight on the front leg with the body open to the ball. These errors in setup and stance move your center ahead of the ball. In order to have the club enter the sand behind the ball you then must shift backward when you should be moving forward. This positioning of the ball too far to the rear also promotes a de-lofting of the club. The results are skulled and/or fat shots.

STANCE AND SETUP

Set the clubface open slightly, and then grip the club. Weaken the grip slightly, that is, move the hands counterclockwise. The V formed by the thumb and index finger on the right hand will move from pointing toward your right shoulder more toward the center of your body. If you want a very high shot, you need to use as much of the back edge of the sole as possible. Set the handle behind the club head—you'll hit the ball higher. Align the shaft perpendicular to the target and face the leading edge to the right of the target.

> *Do not flip the wrists, the ball should come out slowly.*
>
> —*GENE SARAZEN*

Imagine the club swinging up and down, gliding on its back edge through the sand similar to the landing of an airplane.

With the shaft perpendicular to the target line, stand to the handle—that is, point the butt of the clubhead at the center of your body. When you stand to the handle, the ball should be positioned forward in your stance, weight evenly distributed. Dig your feet into the sand, but make sure the sand does not come over the tops of your shoes.

Clubface stays open through impact.

PRE-SWING THOUGHTS

Imagine the club swinging up and down, gliding on its back edge through the sand similar to the landing of an airplane. Let the loft of the club lift the ball. Do not try to lift or scoop the ball.

One final preswing thought: Imagine a smooth and complete throughswing keeping the tempo up throughout.

SWING

Swing the club up more vertically with the arms, leaving the shoulders passive. Keep your weight centered and minimize your turn throughout the backswing. On the throughswing keep the clubface up as the club glides through the sand on its back edge. Enter the sand approximately one to three inches behind the ball. Swing through the shot with your weight finishing on the left side.

GREENSIDE BUNKER SHOT, BALL SITTING UP

Common Mistakes
- Positioning ball too far back in stance
- Hands forward of the ball, de-lofting or using the leading edge of the club
- Failing to keep the club moving completely through the shot

Stance and Setup
- Set the clubface open along the target line
- Weaken the grip slightly (move hands counterclockwise on shaft)
- Align body (feet, legs, shoulders) to the left of the target line
- Point the butt end of the club at the center of your body (stand to the handle)
- Distribute weight evenly

Pre-swing Thoughts
- Think, "Hinge and hold"
- Make smooth downswing and throughswing keeping tempo up throughout
- Let loft of the club lift the ball—do not scoop ball from lie

Swing
- Hinge your wrists in backswing and swing the club up in backswing
- Take club back three-quarters
- Swing club into sand one to three inches behind ball
- Use bottom of club and back edge to splash under ball, keeping heel ahead of toe throughout downswing and impact
- Keep clubhead moving through, up and out of sand while clearing hips to the left of the target line
- Finish with weight on left side

You must get yourself to the point where you can visualize the ball coming out of the bunker, hitting the green at the right spot, and rolling in to the hole. At that point, you'll invariably hit the ball close.
—RAYMOND FLOYD

Fried Egg

HITTING SKY-HIGH APPROACH SHOTS helps stroke a golfer's ego, especially when the ball nose-dives down onto the green and sticks not far from the pin. Suddenly the game seems simpler than it really is. But those towering shots don't always fall from the sky and hit their greens. That can cause problems, particularly when the landing area is a bunker. Chances are, you'll be left with a ball buried in the bunker, commonly referred to as a fried egg for its resemblance to a sunny-side-up egg.

Because you have to hit beneath the ball to lift it out of the bunker, a fried egg presents a problem since half of the ball is below the surface of the sand. Most golfers commonly make one of two mistakes here. Some skull the shot because they've either opened the clubface at address (as they would have for a normal lie in the bunker), or their clubface enters the sand too close to the ball. When the clubface is open, the lead edge is unable to dig deep enough into the sand to lift it out. Entering the sand too close to the ball (less than one-half inch), simply doesn't give the clubhead enough time or space to get beneath the ball.

Others hit far enough behind the ball, but fail to continue swinging the clubhead down the target line. The traditional "V-shaped" swing is not the ideal shape for this shot. Your swing path should more closely resemble a "check-mark" (steep

TAKING YOUR MEDICINE

The fried egg is a tough shot in any ordinary greenside bunker. Facing this lie in a particularly steep bunker is even tougher. Because hitting a fried egg lie produces a low trajectory shot, attempting to play it out of a steep bunker is an ill-advised risk. If you don't have a reasonable chance of clearing the lip of the bunker, you may have to take your medicine and pitch out sideways or even backward. Recognize that there are times on the golf course when playing away from the hole is your best move.

entry followed by a short, low follow-through). Extend through the ball toward the target rather than up toward your shoulders. If you leave the contact area too quickly (dig in and then immediately dig out), the ball may move out of the depression, but it won't escape the bunker. As a result, you'll have a second chance to properly execute a bunker shot.

When faced with a fried egg shot use the digging edge of the club, which will act like a knife cutting down and under the ball.

When this shot is properly executed, the ball will fly on a low trajectory, because it's coming out of a depression. Applying any type of spin is nearly impossible, so be realistic about your goals. If you have a tight pin without a lot of green to work with, the ball is most likely going to run past the hole.

PLAYING THE SHOT

Playing this shot is not as difficult as it appears, especially if you have realistic expectations. First, understand that when faced with a fried egg shot, you want to use the digging edge of the club. The front (or lead) edge of the clubface is for digging while the back edge is the gliding edge used when the ball is sitting on top of the sand. The lead edge acts like a knife and cuts down under the depression that surrounds the ball.

To use the leading edge, press your hands forward to the front edge of the golf ball. This will take some loft off the club so use a 60-degree wedge, which will "net" you approximately 55 or 56 degrees. Using your normal grip, choke down an inch or two. This will put you closer to the ball and make it easier to make your swing more vertical.

Next, stand to handle—that is, center your body to the butt end of the handle of the club. This puts the golf ball back a little in your stance. Using the center of your stance and the rear foot as references, the ball should be in the middle. Playing the ball back slightly and choking down encourages a steeper downswing arc, a necessity for hitting this shot with success.

Your stance should square with approximately 60 percent of your weight on your left side. Adjusting your weight to your forward leg will keep you from raising the clubhead at impact. You must stay down through the shot longer than normal.

Take the club up and back at a steep angle. Keep the legs fairly quiet. Too much leg action can cause you to move backward and skull the shot. Return the club at a steep angle, hitting two to three inches behind the ball. Make sure the club goes down into the sand and underneath the ball. Shorten your follow-through to ensure the club stays down and through the ball. A high follow-through can cause you to "back up," that is, move your body backward during the downswing, thus catching the ball because the back edge of the club hits the sand first. If this happens, you'll skull the shot.

When hit correctly, the ball will pop out, stay low and run after landing on the green. There will be very little (if any) spin, so expect more roll than usual.

Common Mistakes
- Opening the clubface as if you're hitting a sand shot from an ordinary lie
- Clubface enters the sand too shallow and close to the ball
- Breaking into the follow-through too quickly (not giving the club enough time to dig the ball out)
- Swinging the club on a flat (rather than steep) swing path
- Finishing high rather than finishing low

Stance and Setup
- De-loft the club by moving the handle forward of the clubface
- Stand to handle (club handle bisecting an imaginary line that runs through your midsection)
- Lean approximately 60 percent of your weight on your front leg
- Grip down an inch or two on the club
- Play the ball back (one-half to one inch) in your stance

Pre-swing Thoughts
- Think of the lead edge as a knife that cuts beneath the ball to pop it out
- Keep the lower body quiet
- Finish low

Swing
- Swing the club up with the arms and hands; keep the body quiet
- Swing should be steep (V-shaped)
- Abbreviate the follow-through

-No.-
11
...

No bunker shot has ever scared me, and none ever will. The key to this bravado is practice. I've practiced and experimented from hundreds of lies with various swings, in effect creating a data bank in my memory that I can call on no matter what kind of sand shot I'm facing. Just as important, I've developed my imagination to the point that I'm confident I can think my way out of any bunker, no matter how tough the lie.
—GARY PLAYER

Long—30- to 40-Yard— Explosion Shot

WHEN WALTER HAGEN CAME TO THE 15TH HOLE at Royal St. George's Sandwich course in the final round of the 1922 British Open, he needed par on each of the remaining holes to become the first native-born American to win the prestigious event. Then his second shot landed in a bunker—a particularly tough lie, known as Cross Bunker, approximately 45 yards from the pin.

Hagen faced two options: explode the ball with a sand wedge, which would run the risk of coming up short and leave a chip for par. Or he could play a mid-iron (six or seven) or short iron (an eight- or nine-iron or pitching wedge) that would provide enough carry to the green but would be difficult to stop. Hagen studied the shot, vacillating from sand wedge to mid-iron, from mid-iron to wedge. Finally, he settled on the mid-iron.

NOT YOUR GARDEN VARIETY SAND BUNKER SHOT

The mid-iron at least gave him a chance to save par with a putt if he could keep the shot on the putting surface. Should you face a long explosion shot similar to Hagen's, a shot from 30, 40, or even 50 yards, here's how to pull it off.

Use a nine-iron or pitching wedge. Set the clubface slightly open, that is, the face a little wider as you view it from the set up. It should point more skyward and be angled slightly to the right (heel closer to the ball than the toe). When the club is slightly open it will glide on its back edge through the sand at impact. After you've set the clubface, position your hands on the club.

Position the shaft so that it is perpendicular to your intended start line and take a stance that allows the shaft and your grip to point to the middle of the body. Wiggle your feet into the sand to give you a firm footing but not so deep that the sand covers the lips of your shoes.

Swing the club back straight but lower than you would for a normal bunker shot. Use your arms and shoulders, keeping the wrists passive to produce more of an oval-shaped swing. Finish the swing by turning through to the left side facing the target.

When you swing be sure to use the back edge of the club. Let the bottom, or sole, of the club glide through the sand. Splash the ball out just as you would in a greenside sand bunker shot.

American courses, especially in Florida, feature sand scrapes, which are very shallow bunkers that are not very penal. Gaping and dangerous bunkers, such as Oakmont Country Club's Church Pews, are open graves of torture.

—BEN WRIGHT

PICKING THE BALL ON PURPOSE ON 50- TO 70-YARD DISTANCES

When you're 50 to 70 yards from the target you can opt to play a shot that will pick the ball rather than explode it from the sand. Select a pitching wedge and set the face approximately 10 degrees open—this will enable you to play a cut shot. Aim slightly to the left with your stance with the ball a bit forward, pointing the club at the middle of your body. Control the distance of the shot by varying the length of the backswing. At impact contact the ball before the sand and follow through the same length as your backswing.

Those who saw Hagen play agreed that he often performed his best in seemingly hopeless situations. His second shot on Royal St. George's 15th was testimony. He struck the shot, carried the remaining 35 yards onto the green where it rolled to a stop less than a foot from the cup. Hagen made his par putt. Then he made par on each of the final three holes to win the championship by a single stroke.

LONG—30- TO 40-YARD— EXPLOSION SHOT

Common Mistakes

- Using too much wrist and swinging the club too steep into the sand
- Skulling the ball by falling backward at impact

Stance and Setup

- Set clubface slightly open
- Point the club at the center of the body
- Position ball slightly forward of center and assume a slightly open or square stance

In a long explosion shot swing the club back straight but lower than you would for a normal bunker shot.

Pre-swing Thoughts
- Allow for a slight left-to-right ball flight
- Let the sole and back edge of the clubhead splash the sand

Swing
- Swing the club back with the arms and shoulders creating a oval-shaped swing
- Keep the clubface open and gliding, finishing the swing with a full follow-through

-No.- 12

To be really expert in recovering from any kind of trouble, including bunkers, a player must possess a certain amount of ingenuity in addition to a highly developed sense of club control. Many of the shots made from such places are not golf shots at all, but are acts of club manipulation possibly never tried before. The player who can handle his tools and has a spark of inspiration can often do wonders.
—BOBBY JONES

Buried in Deep Bunker, Nearly Under the Lip

WHEN YOU'VE SUNK A BALL UNDER THE LIP of a deep bunker, you have to be ready to make some concessions. Chances are, you're not going to hit a perfect pin shot from here. If you can get the ball on the green, you've done a good job.

Try to do more and you may end up faring worse. When hitting this shot, you won't be able to exert much control over either the flight of the ball or the roll once it lands. Another mistake is to think you can splash the ball on the green—that is, make it fly higher and softer by using the bottom and back edge of the clubhead. It won't work. Rather, you need to dig the ball out with the front edge of your sand wedge, and you have to dig deep and hard.

To execute this difficult recovery shot, begin by planting your feet and getting a stable base. This won't be easy on a severely sloped embankment. Lean your weight into the bank, over the front knee. Then open your stance and position the ball in the middle-to-back part of your stance.

Once you've done that, set your clubface square. Hinge the club quickly with the wrists, creating a steep backswing. On the downswing rotate the toe. Enter the sand about an inch behind the ball. Drive the clubface deep into the bank, all the while

THE CHOPPING ACTION

Stuart Appleby, who is consistently ranked among the top sand bunker players on the PGA Tour, describes the chopping action needed to dislodge a ball in a buried lie:

"With a ball buried in the bunker, the first thing to hope for is that you have plenty of green to work with. If you do not have much green, it does not matter how good you are; you are really going to struggle with this shot. The best thing to do is to open up your stance, put the ball well back, and keep your hands low during your setup.

"What you want is that feel of the club almost getting picked up rather than swung—sort of like a chopping action or chopping a log— and try to come down about an inch behind the ball with the neck of the club. The hosel will cut under the sand, and you'll get a powerful little eruption of sand. You won't have any real follow-through. You are just throwing the club down and using the power and steepness of the angle to get under it as quickly as you can."

rotating the toe so that the clubface closes while moving under and past the ball. Leave the clubface in the sand. This will pop the ball in the air about a foot or so, enough for it to clear the lip and trickle safely onto the green.

This is not a finesse shot, so swing hard and turn your club over forcefully. By keeping the clubface in the sand throughout the shot you will keep from getting hurt, should your club strike the lip of the green. Stay balanced throughout and don't let yourself fall backward. Lean as much as possible into the bank.

When I need to "knife" down and under a buried ball, I go with a square clubface to aid the knifing action, combined with an abrupt upright swing arc.

—JACK NICKLAUS

BURIED IN DEEP BUNKER, NEARLY UNDER THE LIP

Common Mistakes
● Attempting to do too much with the shot—
  think "Get it on the green, somewhere"
● Trying to scoop the ball out versus leaving the club in the sand

Stance and Setup
● Open stance and place ball in middle of stance
  or slightly toward rear foot
● Grip down on club
● Dig feet firmly into sand; lean into slope to maintain
  balance and keep from falling backward
● Rotate toe of club closed through impact
● Keep club in sand on follow-through

A key to hitting this shot is to rotate the toe on the downswing, at impact and while driving the clubface deep into the bank.

Pre-swing Thoughts

- A "good shot" is one that gets the ball onto the green
- Think positively—if sand allowed ball to penetrate its surface it will allow your club to enter and propel the ball out

Swing

- Swing hard but don't lose balance
- Make a steep takeaway and downswing; do not sweep or try to splash the ball onto the green—instead, dig with front edge of the club
- Bury the club in the bank—no follow-through

The common error in this shot is to blade the ball thin into the face of the bunker or over the green. But if you make a point of hitting down hard, then you'll be able to get the wedge under the ball and that action will lift it up over the lip.

—GREG NORMAN

Short, High Shot with Feet Outside, Ball in Greenside Bunker

SEEING YOUR APPROACH SHOT VANISH into a greenside bunker can dash your hopes of making par. Discovering that the ball is resting on the upper edge of the bunker, and that you are now forced to hit a ball below your feet while standing outside the bunker, may leave you wanting to stick your head in the sand, ostrich-style.

Playing this bunker shot is difficult, but not impossible. The most common mistake golfers make is skulling the shot. This usually happens because they come up and out of the shot. It can also result from failing either to (1) steepen the backswing, or (2) tilt forward from the hips and increase their knee flex. Any one of these mistakes spoils the shot.

PLAYING THE SHOT

Hitting a sand shot with your feet outside the bunker places you in a precarious position, so focus on one simple goal—getting the ball out of the bunker. This is

GET A FEEL FOR THE TEXTURE

Variations of sand conditions can turn this extraordinary sand shot into an even tougher one, and a "garden variety bunker shot" into an adventure. Here are some examples of different sand textures and how to adjust your play:

Average (soft) sand. **Open the clubface and apply the normal hinge-back and hold-through method. Take a full swing and finish on the left side.**

Heavy and fluffy sand. **Use a sand wedge with the clubface set more open, thus incorporating the back edge of the club and increasing the bounce. Grip down an inch on the club and play the ball just forward of center in your stance. Swing with more speed as the heavy sand slows the club through impact.**

Hard sand. **Use a lob wedge with less bounce. Set the clubface just slightly open. Make the same swing as you would in normal sand.**

Wet, compacted sand. **Use a lob wedge with the face set to square. Play the ball in the center of your stance. Move your hands slightly ahead of the ball at address. Align your stance parallel to the target line and make your normal bunker swing. Expect a lower trajectory and greater roll.**

your primary concern. Hopefully, lady luck will be on your side and you'll end up with an opportunity to get the ball up and down. But first master the technique of getting the ball out and on the green. Then you can think about getting it close to the pin.

STANCE AND SETUP

Here are the rules for hitting this shot, and some specific adjustments you should make when the sand texture is light, heavy, or wet. Take your grip at the very end of the handle. Weaken the grip slightly (turn your top hand counter-clockwise an inch). This keeps the club from turning over (or closing) before contact and gets the ball up and out. Remind yourself that even though your feet are outside the bunker the ball is in the sand and you can't ground the club at address.

With the ball below your feet, the setup requires a greater forward tilt from the

Remind yourself that even though your feet are outside the bunker the ball is in the sand and you can't ground the club at address.

hips. Keep your feet slightly farther than shoulder-width apart and align them square to the target if possible. Increase your knee flex to lower your center of gravity. This will counterbalance the forward tilt and lower the arc of your swing.

How far you want the ball to carry and the texture of the sand dictate the club-face position. If the pin is close and/or the sand is soft, you want the clubface open. If the pin stands at a greater distance and/or the sand is firm, hit the shot with a very slightly open clubface.

This particular shot calls for a steep "V-shaped" swing. If your swing is too flat, you'll risk coming up out of the shot prematurely and hitting the ball thin (or skulling it). Keep the lower body quiet (nearly still) in the backswing. Do not coil or turn the hips away from the target. With your knees flexed and your legs un-moving, swing your arms down in front of your body.

Your finish should be lower than normal. With a follow-through that is too high and moves around back, you'll lose knee flex, raise up and skull the shot. Follow through low, so your body stays low, and the clubhead contacts the sand behind and beneath the ball. If the pin is very deep or if you have to carry a few feet of grass to reach the green, you can give the swing a little more force, but above all remain in balance. Remember, never swing so hard that you can't maintain your body position.

SHORT, HIGH SHOT WITH FEET OUTSIDE, BALL IN GREENSIDE BUNKER

Common Mistakes

- Not enough forward tilt from the hips
- Not enough flex at the knees
- Swinging too hard
- Come up and out of the shot
- Swing path is too shallow

Stance and Setup
- Hold club at full length
- Spread feet slightly farther than shoulder-width apart
- Increased knee flex
- Forward tilt from the hips
- Align feet square to the target
- Address clubface from square to the target to open based on texture of sand

Pre-swing Thoughts
- Create a steeper than normal swing
- Stay down and low through impact

Swing
- Swing arms up, keep body quiet in backswing
- Swing should be steep (V-shaped)
- Swing club down into sand with arms, keeping body relatively quiet
- Make a low follow-through

There is an old saying: If a man comes home with sand in his cuffs and cockleburs in his pants, don't ask him what he shot.
—SAM SNEAD

Short, High Shot with Downhill Lie in a Greenside Bunker

LPGA LEGEND MICKEY WRIGHT FOUND HERSELF in a tight spot on the 18th hole of the San Diego Country Club in the final round of the 1964 U.S. Women's Open. Wright, a three-time U.S. Women's Open champion, came to the final hole needing a birdie to beat rival Ruth Jessen or a par to tie and force a playoff. But her two-iron approach was clumsy, and found a bunker on the right side of the green of the 395-yard par 4. The ball rested approximately 100 feet away from the pin at the extreme right side of the bunker. Her lie was downhill.

Standing over the ball, Wright saw that if she didn't take enough sand she would sail the ball over the green and if she took too much sand—a common error here —she would leave the ball well short of the hole.

In the end she made the choice that she and you and any other golfer in this situation should make: she swung hard and steep, exploding the ball up and onto the green, stopping it five feet from the cup. She sunk the par-saving putt and forced an 18-hole playoff, in which she shot 70 to Jessen's 72 and claimed her fourth U.S. Women's Open title.

SWING PATH IS CRUCIAL

The most important aspect of hitting a downhill lie in a greenside bunker is the angle you create when hitting the shot. It has to be very steep, yet forceful enough to create a splash. Many players do exactly the opposite, coming into the ball at an angle that is too shallow, catching a piece of the ball with the leading edge of the clubface and skulling it over the green. A steep swing and a club that gives you the maximum height—a lob wedge, if you have one—should prevent this. You must

keep the club moving down and forward as it passes completely under the ball and through the sand. Correctly executed, you should displace more sand in front of the ball than behind it—roughly twice as much. Another important key to this shot is to keep the club open while swinging down so abruptly into the sand. Do not cut the swing off after contacting the sand. Keep the swing moving low and forward and resist the customary high finish of a normal sand bunker shot.

The two mistakes I see most often from amateurs are lifting up and hitting the equator of the ball, sending it into the next county, or taking a divot of sand large enough to bury a cat.

—SAM SNEAD

Add extra loft to counteract the steep angle of the slope—use a lob wedge and take a very steep approach to the ball.

If you keep in mind that hitting firmly into the sand a couple of inches behind the ball will create sufficient pressure to "explode" the ball out of the bunker, half your mental block will be cured. You will cure the other half simply by remembering to hit through the sand without closing the clubface. In other words, follow through without rolling your wrists.

—JACK NICKLAUS

LOSS OF BALANCE

Another difficulty arises from the player's loss of balance. Because gravity is pulling the player down the slope (forward, or to the left), the player often tries to recapture his or her balance, which causes the player to fall back toward the rear or right leg. This can happen just when you need stability and balance the most—as you take the club back. When you lose balance and inadvertently move backward the club swings up too soon and you skull the ball, or you hit too far behind the ball. Either way you've blown the shot.

EXECUTION

When taking your shot, be sure to take an open stance, left foot pulled back from the target line. Position the ball in the center of the body, opposite the sternum. Dig

ADJUST FOR THE SAND CONDITIONS

Sand conditions call for adjustments. If the sand is hard or wet, you need to guard against having the clubhead bounce off the sand and into the ball. With a sand wedge or L-wedge, square up the clubface (which diminishes the bounce of the sole) and make sure you enter the sand with the front edge of the club leading

If the sand is dry and fluffy, avoid digging too far into the sand by opening the clubface and using the back edge. Adjust by gripping down an inch on the grip and stabilize your feet by digging into the sand an inch or two.

in more with the left foot (positioned down the slope). Set your weight on the left side over the left knee. Keep it there throughout the swing. Also, grip your lob wedge weaker than usual. This will keep the club lofted throughout the swing.

Pick up the club with a quick wrist cock and bring it down quickly. The ball flight will be lower than normal because you're swinging downhill. Swing hard—you'll need it to generate the needed carry and loft. To put it another way, give it a good whack and finish the shot with your weight completely on the downhill leg.

SHORT, HIGH SHOT WITH DOWNHILL LIE IN A GREENSIDE BUNKER

Common Mistakes
- Not adjusting for de-lofting effect of club caused by down slope of bunker
- Coming into the ball with an angle that is too shallow
- Losing balance, falling backward while fighting gravity

Stance and Setup
- Take an open stance
- Position ball in center of body, opposite sternum
- Dig in with left foot and set weight on left side over slightly flexed knee

Pre-swing Thoughts
- Swing the club up and down along the contour of the slope
- Keep the clubface open, sliding under the ball
- Allow for roll after ball lands on green

Swing
- Pick up club with a quick wrist cock and bring it back down quickly
- Swing hard but stay under control. If you're losing your balance, make sure you're going forward and not backward

Keep in mind that hitting firmly into the sand a couple of inches behind the ball will create sufficient pressure to "explode" the ball out of the bunker...and remember to hit through the sand without closing the clubface, in other words, without rolling your wrists.
—JACK NICKLAUS

Uphill Lie in a Greenside Bunker

BOB TWAY, IN ONLY HIS SECOND YEAR on the PGA Tour, hit one of golf's most memorable shots from an uphill lie in a greenside bunker. When Tway hit the shot, he and Greg Norman were both just off the green of the 18th hole at Inverness in the 1986 PGA Championship. After 71 holes and two shots on 18, they were tied for the lead.

Norman had driven the fairway and sucked his approach shot back off the green. Tway, who hit in the rough off the tee, bunkered his second shot right off the pin and below the green. Tway's next shot shocked the gallery and millions of fans watching on television. He lofted his ball over the lip and rolled it into the cup for a birdie three. When Norman failed to sink his birdie try, Tway took home the championship.

Tway later spoke about this miraculous shot: "I was only trying to get the ball on the green. I thought if I could get it on the green and hole the putt, I could force a tie with Greg Norman. I set up to the shot pretty much square and took the club back just a little outside. I tried to make a nice swing and let the explosion of the clubface through the sand throw the ball up onto the green. The key to that is that

*I'll never forget the
bunker shot I holed out on the
16th hole of my singles match at the
1995 Ryder Cup at Oak Hill. I was three
down with three to go, and I was lying two in
the greenside bunker. My opponent was two feet
from the hole and lying three. The ball was resting
on a little bit of an upslope. When you have that
lie in the bunker, as long as the ball isn't plugged,
you can swing with confidence because you know
the slope will help lift the ball into the air. In that
case I probably carried it a little farther than I
wanted to, but it hopped into the hole
on the first bounce.*

—JAY HAAS

you have to follow through. You cannot just stick the club in the sand and hope the ball pops out. The only way you are going to get that explosion is if the club keeps on moving through the sand."

No one is thrilled when faced with hitting from an uphill lie out of a greenside bunker. Some golfers are mentally defeated even before they've hit the shot; they let negative thoughts flood their mind. "I'm either going to skull this and send it flying over the green or hit it fat and dump it right back at my feet," are the kinds of self-defeating thoughts that raise anxiety and exacerbate technical flaws.

The truth of the matter is that bunker play doesn't have to be such an ordeal. With an understanding of the proper technique and a little practice you should be able to escape routinely with a single shot, even knock it close to the pin. Just as Tway successfully made his championship-winning shot by keeping the club moving through the sand, so should you. And the uphill lie will help you to stop the ball close to where it lands.

When hitting an uphill greenside bunker shot keep in mind that the slope of the bunker is adding loft to the shot.

SLOPE ADDS LOFT

When hitting an uphill greenside bunker shot keep in mind that the slope of the bunker is adding loft to the shot. So forget about using a more lofted lob wedge—the 56- or 54-degree sand wedge is right for the job. And don't make the mistake of manipulating the club too much—for instance, don't open your clubface as much as you might for other bunker shots. Because of the slope you don't need the added height that a fully open face would give you. However, you should very slightly open the clubface, just enough so that the leading edge doesn't dig in to the sand. The combination of the upward slope and swinging through the sand will cause the ball to pop out nicely, just as Bob Tway's did.

Align yourself with a slightly open stance. However, narrow it and play the ball in the center. Set the clubface square to very slightly open. The most critical aspect of your stance and setup is keeping your weight on the left side. Gravity will pull you back and down the slope. To compensate, dig your feet two or three inches into the sand, leaning into the slope. Place your weight over a flexed front knee and keep it on the front side throughout the swing. As you lean your left knee toward

10 COMMANDMENTS OF BUNKER PLAY

1. The shorter and higher you want the ball to fly, the more you should open your clubface in relation to the target.

2. The longer and lower you want the ball to fly, the more you should square the clubface to the target.

3. The shorter and higher you want the ball to fly, the more you should hinge the club in the backswing.

4. The longer and lower you want the shot to fly, the less you should hinge the club in the backswing.

5. The shorter and higher you want the ball to fly, the weaker you should position your grip.

6. The longer and lower you want the ball to fly, the less you adjust your grip (take normal grip).

7. The shorter and higher you want the ball to fly, the deeper you should dig your feet into the sand.

8. The longer and lower you want the ball to fly, the less you should dig your feet into the sand.

9. The faster you swing, the more velocity the shot will have, which means the effects of your adjustments will be more magnified.

10. The slower you swing, the less velocity the shot will have, which means the effects of your adjustments are diminished.

the target make sure to keep your shoulders parallel to the slope. This will keep the club from digging in to the sand.

Swing aggressively. Enter the sand fairly close to the ball, no more than one to one and one-half inches behind it. The ball will fly very high, perhaps as much as 75 to 80 degrees, and roll very softly upon landing.

Common Mistakes
- Selecting a club with added loft, such as a lob wedge
- Failing to carry the ball well onto the green close to the pin (there is minimal roll after landing on green)
- Failing to keep the weight on the forward leg through impact

Stance and Setup
- Align feet slightly open to target line and narrow stance slightly
- Set shoulders parallel to slope
- Set clubface square to slightly open behind the ball and along the target line
- Set weight over flexed left (forward) knee

Pre-swing Thoughts
- Remember to keep weight on your forward leg throughout swing
- Swing along slope of bunker

Swing
- Enter sand close to ball, one to one and one-half inches behind it
- Swing aggressively but maintain balance
- Complete follow through, do not leave club buried in sand

The sand shot is one of the most forgiving shots in golf. Just knowing that will decrease your anxiety when you step into a bunker.
—NICK PRICE

Ball Above Feet on Bunker Slope

WHILE BUNKER SHOTS MAY BE EASY for tour players who have mastered the correct techniques, they remain among the most difficult for the average golfer. One in particular, the bunker shot off a slope with the ball above the feet, calls for adjustments that don't come automatically. The swing characteristics of most amateur golfers include (1) slight out-to-in swing path, (2) steep rather than shallow arc through the impact zone, and (3) a tendency to hit off the back foot (reverse pivot). Every one of these movements must be eliminated when hitting a ball above your feet in a sand bunker.

The most common mistake is failing to adjust the swing plane. When the ball is above your feet you must shorten the club by gripping down, because the ball is actually closer to you. And you must swing more "around" the body, much like a baseball swing. A steep swing plane just gets you into trouble. The club enters the sand at an angle that gathers too much sand between the ball and the clubface to propel the ball out of the bunker.

Moving the club from outside the target line to inside—that is, cutting across the ball—is often the cause of this steep approach. The problem looms when you approach this shot as if it were a normal lie in the bunker. The key is to change the path of the swing to a flatter arc—one that matches the slope on which the ball rests.

STANCE AND SETUP

The adjustments for the swing start with the stance and setup. Stand taller with the knees flexed. Set your spine angle closer to perpendicular, chin off chest. Align your feet parallel to the target line. Dig your feet in slightly and set the club open to the target line. The amount you open the clubface should be relative to how far you want the ball to carry. Grip down on the handle. Position the ball in the middle of the stance. You want to make sure you don't enter the sand too far behind the ball.

The height of a bunker shot will be regulated by one's ability to displace the sand upward. . .the direction, by one's ability to displace sand toward the target.

—CHRIS RILEY

PRE-SWING THOUGHTS

Think "around the body" for takeaway and through swing and keep the clubface in the same position through impact as was set at address. The position of the clubface is critical—make sure the clubface stays open, gliding on its back edge through impact.

THE SAND WEDGE— HOW TO LET THIS TOOL WORK FOR YOU

The flange or back edge of the sand wedge keeps the leading edge from digging too deeply into the sand. It rides through, more or less, horizontally. Let this thick sole work for you—when it displaces the sand as it enters it gives the ball a cushion to ride on. Don't switch off the power just when it needs a lift up and out—keep your clubhead moving through, out and up.

For the most part, players need to swing more aggressively in the sand because the sand slows down the clubhead through impact. However, it is important to keep the acceleration smooth and rhythmical, not quick and jerky.

Stand taller with the knees flexed and set the clubface open according to how far you want the ball to carry.

SWING

Exaggerate the flatness of the swing. Do not release the club around the back-side. Rather, keep it moving more down the target line. Don't let your right hand roll closed; keep the palm of your right hand matched (parallel) to the face of the club. Here is a visual image to help you from closing the face prematurel—picture balancing a glass of water on the clubface, without spilling it, until well into the follow-through.

Coil your body onto the back leg. Uncoil it to the forward leg and finish the swing, keeping the club in front of the body through the impact area. Overall, make a rhythmic pass—don't add any "hit" at impact.

······· **BALL ABOVE FEET ON BUNKER SLOPE** ··················

Common Mistakes
- Failing to swing around body and approach ball
  with shallow swing arc
- Failing to move ball closer to middle of stance
- Failing to keep the clubface open and gliding through the sand

Stance and Setup
- Stand taller with knees flexed
- Grip down on club
- Position ball in the middle or just ahead of middle of stance

Pre-swing Thoughts
- Think "around the body" for takeaway and through swing
- Maintain open-faced position of clubface

Swing
- Exaggerate the flatness of the swing
- Keep club in front of the body and the clubface lofted through impact (no release)
- Make a rhythmic pass and don't add "hit" at impact
- Finish facing the target

Harvey Penick always wanted us to be good bunker players so we wouldn't be afraid to fire at a flag tucked next to one.
—BEN CRENSHAW

Wet, Compacted Sand

GOOD RESULTS FROM A SAND BUNKER, like good results on the putting green, depend greatly on your ability to "read the sand," much as you would "read the green." Use your feet and eyes. Walking to the ball and assuming your stance will give you opportunities to learn about the sand's depth, its degree of firmness (fluffy or packed), and whether it is coarse or granular, dry or wet. If the sand is coarse or wet it will also be firmer, which will cause more bounce upon the club's entry. If the sand is fluffy or dry, your club will dig and slide more easily under the ball. For a ball on soft sand, use more of the back edge (bounce) of your club. For a ball resting on wet sand, use the leading edge of your club to dig.

Failing to use the leading edge of the club is one of the most common mistakes made when hitting from a wet sand bunker.

Varying the depth of the cut and the speed of the swing can control distance. If you make a deeper cut, the ball will fly shorter and higher. If you make a shallower cut, the ball will fly longer and lower. Vary the depth of the cut by hinging the club up in the backswing. For a shallower cut, use less hinge in the backswing. A slower swing will cut down distance just as a faster swing will add carry. An easy way to regulate the speed or force of your swing is to focus on varying the length of your follow-through. A shorter follow-through will cut down on the distance of the shot while a longer one will carry the ball farther.

If you use the back edge of the sand wedge, the club will tend to bounce off the firm surface and strike the ball with the leading edge of the club, causing a skulled shot.

STANCE AND SETUP

Here's how to set up for the shot. Assume a square or slightly open stance. Dig in the feet until you have a firm foundation and good balance. Lean slightly toward the target. Grip down on the club, that is, turn your hands more toward the target. Square or set the clubface perpendicular to the target line. Select an entry spot for the leading edge of the club approximately two inches behind the ball.

SWING

Swing back to three-quarters, hinging the club up in front of the body. Drop the club down into the sand and dig under the ball. Keep the club leading the body through impact. Finish the shot with your weight on the front leg.

You can use this same swing and stance not only for the sand wedge but also for a lob wedge, nine-iron or eight-iron and thus have several distances in your shot repertoire.

It is hard to judge the strength or thickness of the sand—a very important matter—because you are not allowed to touch the sand with your club. However, you can plant your feet firmly in the sand when addressing the ball, and after a little experience you will be able to estimate the strength of the sand by means of a pair of well-trained feet.

—JEROME TRAVERS

Failing to use the leading edge of the club is one of the most common mistakes made when hitting from wet sand.

WET, COMPACTED SAND

Common Mistakes

- Failing to pay attention to the texture of the sand when digging in your feet
- Failing to use the leading edge of the club to dig in to the sand

Stance and Setup

- Set the clubface square to the target line
- Lean toward the target
- Dig feet into the sand

Pre-swing Thoughts

- Make certain that leading edge of club digs into sand
- Use speed and force of swing, depth of cut or both to vary distance
- Allow for ball to come out faster

Swing

- Hinge the club steeply on the backswing
- Take club back three-quarters
- Maintain tempo

One of the easiest ways to add height to the sand shot is to feel like you're sitting down on your right knee at address. You should widen your stance and choke up a little. You should feel as if you're "under" the ball more and have a wider base.
—BEN CRENSHAW

Sand Bunker Shot to Elevated Green

IF YOU EVER HAD THE OPPORTUNITY to play in Scotland or Ireland, where a bunker is often a true penalty, you have to learn to elevate the ball quickly and after hitting the green stop suddenly. This is one of the classiest shots in golf. It really excites the fans.

Paul Azinger has heard the cheers. In 1993, he holed an elevated greenside bunker shot on the 72nd hole in the Memorial Tournament to defeat Corey Pavin by one stroke and Payne Stewart by two. In 2002, he holed another greenside bunker shot at The Belfry in the Ryder Cup matches to halve his match with Niclas Fasth.

REMEMBER THREE THINGS

The type of shot you play from a greenside bunker is predicated on three things: the lie of the ball, the severity of the face of the bunker (that is, the height of the lip or the top edge of the bunker), and the distance from your ball to the hole. The typical bunker shot requires you to play from a clean lie, over a moderate lip, to a hole that is far enough away that you can make an aggressive swing. The shot from a deep bunker to an extremely elevated green is different entirely—it requires some important adjustments.

The key to hitting this shot is to dispense all of the clubhead's energy just behind the ball and into the sand, thus forcing the ball up quickly.

The key to this shot is quick elevation combined with a lot of spin. The keys to elevation and spin are a steep angle, maximum loft, and greater-than-average swing speed. The common mistake players make when faced with this shot is they don't have the correct amount of any of these elements. Most often players revert to try to scoop the ball over a tall lip by falling backward trying to get the ball into the air. The outcome is typically a bladed shot that hits the lip and comes back into the bunker or a fat shot that doesn't carry over the bunker.

GET ELEVATED

The first key to elevation is to swing down into the sand versus up toward the sky. The key to swinging down is lowering your hands by bending over at the hips. At the same time turn the face wide open so that it is looking up at you versus the target. Always remember to open the face first. Then grip the club and keep the handle behind the ball. Stand to the handle, that is, point the butt end of the shaft to the center of your body. Your stance should be more open than usual and the ball placement should be even with your forward toe. Add more knee flex to support your weight. Tilt slightly forward.

After you have set up properly, start the club in motion by hinging the wrists immediately off the ball, creating a vertical takeaway. Depending on how far you

When you are digging your feet in to play a bunker shot, especially if it is your first one of the day, you should be paying attention to two things: You should dig deep enough and you should note the texture of the sand. The texture of the sand has a big effect on the shot. In hard sand, the ball is going to come out faster, because the club is going to bounce off the harder surface and increase the velocity of the shot.

—GIL MORGAN

need to carry the ball, add commensurate arm swing. However, your body should not move off the ball. Swing the club down into the sand vertically. Maintain maximum loft through impact. The idea is to dispense all your energy just behind the ball and into the sand, thus forcing the ball up quickly on the cushion of displaced sand. The follow-through will be shorter and abbreviated while the body remains centered.

SHOT BRIEFS

SAND BUNKER SHOT TO ELEVATED GREEN

Common Mistakes
- Shallow approach, trying to scoop the ball into the air
- Not enough loft at address
- Ball too far back in the stance, with hands behind the ball

Stance and Setup
- Open the face aggressively, with the handle behind the ball
- Take grip after face is set open
- Tilt more toward from the hips, lowering hands
- Take stance with more knee flex, playing the ball off the forward toe

Swing

- Swing the club up abruptly by hinging the wrists immediately
- Allow arms to finish the backswing depending on how far you need to carry the ball
- Swing the club down into the sand, keeping the loft on the face
- Weight should stay centered throughout impact, with a checkmark finish

BUNKER BASICS

I'd like to provide a few general principles of play from the sand that are worth remembering, regardless of the type of shot.

- **Secure your balance by digging one-half inch into the sand with your feet. This not only improves your set up and stance but provides feedback on the consistency of the sand.**
- **The finer the sand, the less the resistance. . .thus, the slower the swing. Conversely, the heavier the sand, the faster the swing.**
- **In all explosions shots, enter the sand behind the ball.**

NOTHING

IS

IMPOSSIBLE

A scorer hones unusual shots on the practice range, or takes time during practice rounds to experiment with extreme measures like water shots or the backhander from the trees.
—RAY FLOYD

Restricted Backswing

AT THE 1984 BRITISH OPEN, the two greatest players in the world at the time—Tom Watson and Seve Ballesteros—were deadlocked at 11-under par with two holes to play in the final round. Ballesteros, who was playing one hole ahead of Watson, saved par on the infamous 17th hole at the Old Course in St. Andrews, also known as the Road Hole. Watson approached the tee knowing he had to make par to keep pace with his Spaniard competitor.

The Road Hole is heralded as one of (if not the) toughest holes in golf. A deep bunker looms to the left of the green and a road backed by a stone out-of-bounds wall stands to the right. These elements make a long second shot hazardous. Watson stepped up to the tee and blistered his shot down the middle of his fairway. He had approximately 200 yards to the pin, and deliberated over hitting his two- or three-iron. He opted to hit the two-iron and pushed the shot long to the right. The ball bounced over the road and off the wall, coming to rest along the wall and leaving him with nearly no room to swing his club. Watson's quest for a sixth British Open title was hanging by a thread.

WHAT YOU CAN AND CAN'T MOVE

It's important for golfers to understand when relief is allowed and to what extent that relief is permitted. Equally important is knowing when you're not allowed to intercede with an obstruction or receive relief. Golfers are often unsure whether they can move a pine cone, bend a branch, push down high grass, or take a club's-length drop from an obstruction. Here's how it breaks down under USGA rules.

A player shall not improve, or allow to be improved, the position of the ball, the area of his intended swing, or his line of play or a reasonable extension of that line beyond the hole or the area in which he is to drop or place a ball by any of the following actions: moving, bending, or breaking anything fixed (including movable obstructions and objects defining out of bounds) or removing or pressing down sand, loose soil, replaced divots, other cut turf placed in position or other irregularities of surface. This applies unless it restricts the golfer from fairly taking his stance or in making a stroke or the backward movement of his club for a stroke.

How does this translate onto the golf course? Well, it's clear under most circumstances that you're not permitted to touch your ball or anything obstructing the path of your swing. This means that you can't break off a branch that is restricting your backswing, and when playing out of native grass you can't stomp your feet and use your club to mat down the grass surrounding your ball.

You are permitted, however, to slightly manipulate an obstruction if it does not allow you to fairly take a stance. If your ball is under a bush, it's okay use your body to push the bush back if that's absolutely necessary to positioning your feet in the stance. Your backswing may still be restricted, but you can at least get a club on the ball.

Even this exception has boundaries. Say you use your back side to back into a small tree, but a branch near your shoulders makes it impossible to swing the club. You cannot grab that branch and "hook" it onto something so it no longer impedes your swing. The rules are a bit subjective, but are effective when practicing common sense.

A LITTLE COMMON SENSE

Restricted backswings can crop up almost anywhere on a golf course: (1) trees (branches) or bushes, (2) out-of-bounds fences or walls or even (3) rocks. Each can present situations for which you're unable to take your normal swing.

The use of common sense is critical when planning your attack. Before setting up to attempt that miracle shot that could save your round, honestly assess the situation. Make sure that you have a shot, and also that you're not risking injury. Check for thick roots or rocks lodged in the ground before slamming your club into the turf. The last thing you want to do is hurt yourself when you could have simply taken an unplayable lie and a one-stroke penalty.

The typical approach of a golfer confronted with a restricted backswing is to take a series of practice swings. Because he's unable to execute his normal swing, he attempts to get comfortable hitting the ball with an atypical swing. However, unless he's careful he can easily revert back to his standard swing when it's time to hit the ball. He'll either come in contact with the obstruction, or mis-hit the ball.

When faced with a restricted backswing accept the reduced width of the swing arc and the result that this swing will bring.

TIME TO EXPERIMENT

When faced with a restricted backswing, first determine the freedom of your backswing and forward swing. To do so, take a few slow practice swings to discover how far you can go. Be careful not to break a branch or move anything during the practice swings because it will draw a one-stroke penalty.

Once you've established how far you can swing, accept this swing arc and the result the swing will bring. You don't always need to fully recover, but you do need to recover. Experiment. Grip down to shorten the arc. Change the plane to suit the situation: a shallower or more vertical approach to avoid striking the obstacle in the path of the normal swing arc. Depending on where the obstruction stands, you can sometimes flatten the swing, but you then must allow for a draw.

Keep your tempo smooth. Many players swing quickly and extra hard in an effort to maximize the distance of the limited swing. Accept what the abbreviated backswing gives you.

ONE APPROACH

I've found the key to hitting a good shot with a restricted backswing is to concentrate on creating more leverage by hinging the wrists earlier in the backswing. This produces additional power. Take more club and set the clubface square. Grip down an inch or two to shorten the club (and thus, the arc) and avoid the obstruction. Move your hands slightly ahead of the ball to allow for greater wrist-action in your swing.

To start this shot, distribute your weight evenly. In your backswing cock your wrists earlier than normal to generate clubhead speed. As you are setting the club, turn your upper body back (or coil) for additional power. Once you've reached the peak of your restricted backswing, smoothly accelerate the clubhead to the ball. Do not surge. Accept the distance the shorter swing gives you.

Whether you're hitting the ball onto the green or down the fairway, allow for some roll. The swing restrictions will produce a lower trajectory shot that will run. Unfortunately, this is something Watson was not able to control. His shot hit the green but rolled 30 feet from the hole. In the end, he missed a par putt. It would have been for naught anyway: Just before he hit the shot, Ballesteros upped the ante, sinking a 15-foot birdie putt on the 18th green. Watson missed par on the next hole too and lost a classic battle by two strokes.

 SHOT BRIEFS ···· **RESTRICTED BACKSWING** ·····

Common Mistakes
- Trying to do too much (hit a heroic shot) instead of trying to recover
- Quick downswing in an effort to hit the ball farther

Stance and Setup
- Determine the freedom of your backswing and forward swing with slow practice swings
- Take more club
- Grip down an inch or two
- Move your hands slightly ahead of the ball
- Distribute weight evenly

Pre-swing Thoughts
- Focus on getting the ball out to safety; you need to recover
- Accelerate the clubhead smoothly in the downswing

Swing
- Hinge the wrists earlier than normal
- Coil (turn your upper body) to generate more power
- Finish low and through

When I hit a shot into trouble, I expect the worst. . .When I get there and find that I can actually hit the ball—which you usually can— it changes my mood for the better right away.
—COREY PAVIN

Opposite-Hand Shot

COREY PAVIN'S ATTITUDE toward trouble shots is excellent. He's got a shot, whatever it might be, and he's going to make the best of it and move on. Should you find yourself in a situation where it is impossible for you to stand and swing normally, consider an opposite-handed swing, or even a one-handed reverse shot. Either could save the day.

THE OPPOSITE WAY

If you opt to swing opposite-handed, make sure you avoid a common mistake: failing to turn the clubface completely on its toe, grooves vertical. This automatically sets the hands in the correct position at address—in the middle of the body opposite the sternum. It will keep them slightly ahead of the ball at impact as well, which will give you the best chance for solid contact.

Select a club with a larger, deeper face, such as a seven-, eight-, or nine-iron. Move closer to the ball and stand the toe of the club on end, grooves facing up and down. This will allow your hands to rest in the middle of your stance, or perhaps slightly forward of the middle. Do not set the hands too far forward, such as in front of the right leg.

Back off and take several practice swings. Practice swings provide kinesthetic

HITTING THE ONE-HANDED REVERSE SWING RECOVERY SHOT

This shot is really not that difficult. It is best used when you cannot address the ball from your normal hitting side, you don't feel comfortable hitting the ball opposite-handed, and you have a short distance to your targeted landing area. Here's what to do.

1. Select a seven-, eight-, or nine-iron.

2. Stand with you back to the target, feet shoulder width apart.

3. Position the ball alongside your right foot, the tip of your toe aligned with the back of the ball.

4. Set the club so that the heel of the clubface is angled slightly off the ground and the ball is centered between the middle of the club and the toe.

5. Grip down on the club, almost to the metal part of the shaft, and position the upper handle to the outside of your lower arm. This will allow the handle to swing freely as you hinge the wrist in the follow-through of the swing.

6. Glance back over your right shoulder at where you want to land the ball.

7. Hinge the club up at the wrist. The backswing (taken in front of your body in the direction you're facing) should be approximately waist high or slightly higher (15 to 20 degrees). Make a full extension of the wrist on the through swing and follow-through. The clubhead should swing almost straight down the target line.

cues—cues that build up the correct swing feelings and actions through physical motion. Swinging a club from the opposite side is new. The brain makes a "quick study" of what's necessary in order for you to hit the ball from the opposite side and helps you make the proper swing. These are important for two reasons. Because swinging from the opposite side itself is new, you need to feel how your body will move during the swing. And the practice swings will enable you to get the feel—and actual location—of where your swing naturally bottoms out. In most instances, this will be slightly back of the mid-point of your stance. Position the ball at this point.

KNOW YOUR GOAL

However, before you move up to your address position and attempt the shot take a moment to consider exactly what you're trying to accomplish. Are you knocking the ball 10 to 15 yards laterally to simply get back in play (a low-risk shot that costs a stroke but gets you restarted in the right direction on the next shot)? Are you trying to keep the shot low, perhaps below some tree branches? Are you trying to run the ball onto the green from a spot alongside a greenside tree, or trying to make a big-time, 50-yard recovery shot down toward the green, or even onto the green?

Make sure it's clear in your mind exactly what you're attempting. Be realistic. Don't overreach in this situation. When in this kind of predicament, remember that recovery is your primary objective. Think, "Recover (first shot) and get well (shot after recovery)." If you try to do too much, you won't accomplish much of anything.

KEEP THAT SWING IN CHECK!

Unless you are a very accomplished player it is best to keep this shot under control, so take a half swing and a follow-through that matches the backswing length.

*When in this kind of predicament, think, "Recover (first shot) and get well (shot after recovery)."
Be realistic and you'll succeed.*

Keep the clubface square at impact. An overactive top hand that shuts the face of the club at impact will cause you to dribble the ball right of your target line. Keep the palm of the top hand square, that is, aligned and parallel with the edge of the toe. Swing with balance and concentrate on solid contact, not power, height, or distance.

Note: It helps to take a few moments on the practice range to swing opposite-handed from time to time. Experiment with different clubs. Learn the flight pattern and length of the shots. Set limits for the distances you hit each club. Build kinesthetic feeling for the swing and refresh it from time to time.

Practice swings will enable you to get the feel—and actual location—of where your swing naturally bottoms out.

In most instances, this will be slightly back of the mid-point of your stance. Position the ball at this point.

 OPPOSITE-HAND SHOT

Common Mistakes
- Failing to turn the clubface completely on its toe, groove vertical
- Trying to overreach with the shot

Stance and Setup
- Move closer to the ball
- Switch your hands on the grip
- Set hands ahead of ball, centered opposite sternum, or slightly forward of center
- Position ball back of center

Pre-swing Thoughts
- Think, "Recover, then get well"
- Select and focus on nature of shot
- Rehearse swing to ingrain kinesthetic feel

Swing
- Take a half swing, back and through
- Keep top hand square, or parallel to clubface
- Swing easy, make solid contact

If you are in the woods, don't act like a seamstress. Your job is not to thread needles but to get the ball back into the fairway.
—ARNOLD PALMER

Under or Through Trees

IN THE FINAL ROUND of the 1954 U.S. Open at Baltusrol in Springfield, New Jersey, Ed Furgol faced the task of getting the ball back into the fairway, except in this case there was an unusual wrinkle. The fairway was an adjoining one on another 18 holes at Baltusrol. The closing holes of Baltusrol's Upper and Lower courses run parallel, separated by a stream lined with tall trees. The 18th hole on the Lower Course, the Open course, has a slight dogleg left.

As Furgol stepped to the 18th tee he led the tournament by a single stroke. He decided to drive to the left side of the fairway to cut some distance to the green, and perhaps get into position to reach it in two shots, but he hooked the shot into the trees. He surveyed the situation. One avenue of escape was a short pitch to the right onto the 18th fairway, which would leave him two shots from the green.

Another escape, however, seemed more likely to yield a par. This was to go left and slightly forward onto the 18th fairway of the Upper Course. The shot would be through a tunnel formed by the canopy of the trees. He envisioned a shot that would rise several feet and no higher, staying low enough to pass through out onto the 18th fairway of the Upper Course. From there, he would have a clear shot, an estimated 150 yards, to the 18th green on the Lower Course. After checking with tournament officials and confirming that his targeted landing area was not out of

> *Making a par after chipping out of the trees can destroy an opponent. Taking a double or triple bogie after hacking your way out of the woods can destroy you.*
>
> **—FRANCISCO LOPEZ**

bounds, he elected to punch an eight-iron through and under the trees.

Furgol rifled his recovery shot cleanly through the woods, then hit a seven-iron just short of the green. He chipped up to five feet and holed his putt for par. The bold play and clutch up-and-down saved his one-stroke lead and, ultimately, the championship.

A WALK IN THE WOODS

Players who try to make shots like Ed Furgol's low-flying, woods-defying masterpiece often make critical mistakes. The most egregious one is, you'll be surprised to learn, not a matter of swing or power but a matter of ball placement; namely putting the ball too far back in the stance. This creates too much shaft angle at impact. It also promotes "backing up" to the ball, that is,

This shot is all about control and solid contact. Take two or three clubs more than normal, grip down one or two inches and maintain a smooth tempo.

moving to the rear in the downswing. At best you'll chunk the shot. At worst, you'll create a reverse pivot and scoop the ball into the overhanging trees.

Of course, club choice is also a concern—you must be certain of your trajectory. If you are unsure of the initial trajectory that a certain club will produce, lay the club on the ground with the face pointing up and the grip pointing toward your target. Step on the clubface until the back of the club is flat on the ground. The angle of the shaft while you are stepping on the club is the approximate trajectory of the ball.

Generally speaking, you'll want to take two or three irons more than normal. For example, use a four-iron or five-iron for a normal seven-iron distance. You will need the extra distance of the stronger club to compensate for an abbreviated swing and choked grip.

Narrow your stance and position the ball in the center of your stance. This will give the shaft an angle at impact that is closer to perpendicular, allowing the club to scrape the ground through impact. Forward pressing the club with the ball back in the stance creates too much angle, forcing the clubhead to dig and mis-hit the shot. Grip down one or two inches on the shaft.

DRIVE YOUR WAY OUT OF TROUBLE

The driver or three-wood can be secret weapons when you need to hit a recovery shot low—such as under low-hanging tree branches—for a long way. It is especially helpful on a par 5 when a long-distance recovery shot—after an errant tee ball—will leave you playing your approach shot to the green in regulation.

The shot will have very little loft and a lot of roll. Under most conditions you can move the ball 160 to 185 yards. Here's how to play it.

1. Grip down on the club two or three inches.

2. Position the ball in the center or slightly forward of center (one-half inch to one inch); open the clubface slightly to increase the loft a few degrees.

3. Align left of the target and allow for a left-to-right movement of 10 to 15 yards.

4. If in the rough hover the club and keep it moving along the top of the grass on the backswing.

5. Make a half to three-quarter backswing then finish low, with your weight fully on the left side.

THINK CLEARING THOUGHTS

This shot is all about control and solid contact. Your club selection has already provided the confidence that you can reach the target. Now you need to concentrate on making a balanced and controlled pass at the ball. Step back and take a few rehearsal swings. Think, "Smooth and easy."

When you shoot, take the club back to three-quarters, hands about shoulder height. Finish low with weight fully on the left side. This will help you cover the golf ball with the clubface at impact.

Common Mistakes
- Trying the heroic shot
- Playing the ball too far back in stance
- Misjudging the trajectory of the shot
- Failing to add two or three clubs

Stance and Setup
- Narrow the stance
- Position the ball in the middle of the stance
- Grip down on the club
- Stand closer to the ball

Pre-swing Thoughts
- Take avenue of escape or recovery that presents least risk and greatest chance for success
- Think, "Tempo, solid contact and finish low"

Swing
- Take it back to a three-quarter length "top" and make a normal turn onto your back leg
- Trap the ball with the clubface, staying on your left side through impact

The primary reason players often make spectacular trouble shots, causing the ball to go under, around, and over obstacles, is that they work harder on visualizing these shots than on those from less demanding positions.
—GARY WIREN

Over a Tree

THE KEY TO HITTING A SHOT OVER A TREE is familiarity. If you are familiar with the trajectories of your clubs and know how your balls usually fly, you'll know how to adjust to nail this shot. If you don't know, you're as likely to hit a bird's nest as a birdie.

Knowing the graduated trajectories for each of the clubs is not common, everyday knowledge among most golfers. These shots are seldom practiced and rarely encountered, so you sometimes have to put your finger to the wind and swing away. However, an effective shortcut, mentioned in the previous chapter, is to lay the chosen club on the ground with the face pointing up and the grip pointing toward the target. Step on the clubface until the back of the club is flat on the ground. The angle of the shaft while you are stepping on the club is the approximate trajectory of the ball.

Once you've done that, factor in your swing style. If it's more like Paul Azinger's boring low trajectory, make adjustments by taking a greater club. If you naturally elevate your shots like Tiger Woods, you should be fine; go ahead and hit the shot if your "field test" has shown you've got enough trajectory to clear the obstacle. Most important, make your swing as if the obstacle doesn't exist.

LOFT AMBITIONS

If you still need to add some loft, there are other adjustments you can make. When you set up, move the ball forward one-ball width (approximately two inches) from its normal position in your stance, leaving the hands in the same position as normal. This will add approximately four degrees of loft to the clubface. Open the face and stance slightly to play a cut shot, which will fly higher than normal. After you've made the setup adjustments, hinge the club up a little more steeply than normal in the backswing. Swing through the shot in the downswing but leave a little more weight on the back leg. Swing the club up to a high finish.

When hitting the ball high, it's important to uncock the wrists a little earlier than they would in playing a normal shot. The idea is to bring the clubhead into the ball slightly on the upswing. This technique results in more height to the flight of the ball.

—BYRON NELSON

ANOTHER CHOICE: THE PUNCH SHOT

In some instances, you might be better served by going under a tree that stands in your way. If so, try hitting a punch shot, which can travel upwards of 100 yards, depending on the club selected. Here's what to do:

1. Select a less lofted club, usually a long iron or a mid-iron (three-, four-, or five-iron).
2. Plan on carry and roll when visualizing the shot.
3. Aim for the highest gap under the branches.
4. Set up square to the target and position the ball in the middle of your stance, or even an inch back of middle.
5. Grip down on the club approximately two inches and stand closer to the ball, weight evenly distributed.
6. Cock your wrists early and take your hands back to waist high or slightly above the waist (10 o'clock).
7. Swing the clubhead through the ball and finish with a low, abbreviated follow-through (about waist level or slightly higher).

Remember, the most common mistakes with this shot are failure to judge the needed elevation correctly and hitting the ball with the front edge of the clubface, that is, "blading it" and rocketing it along the ground. When in doubt about the trajectory, always take a club that will give you added loft. To avoid blading the ball, concentrate on swinging through the shot and trust the loft of the club.

·······**OVER A TREE**··

Common Mistakes
- Failure to correctly judge the needed elevation. Always select a club that will provide added height to the trajectory. Your first objective is to move beyond the obstacle
- Blading the shot because of trying to lift the ball versus trusting the loft of the club to lift the ball

Stance and Setup
- Position the ball opposite the instep of the left foot
- Open the clubface if added height is needed

To avoid blading this shot, concentrate on swinging through the shot and trust the loft of the club.

● Align feet, shoulders, chest slightly open to the target line

Pre-swing Thoughts
● Ask yourself, "Will this club accomplish the primary objective, to get over the obstacle?"
● Ask yourself, "Is my natural ball flight helping or hindering this shot?"
● Swing the club through the ball and let the club do the work; trust the plan, the club, and your swing

Swing
● Hinge the club up more directly in the backswing
● Swing through impact to a high finish
● Finish on the forward leg

SECTION IV

DOWN THE FAIRWAY

It's no accident that some of the best drivers in the game have used the fade as their bread-and-butter shot. Sam Snead, Ben Hogan, Jack Nicklaus, and Lee Trevino, just to name a few, are among the most accurate drivers in history, and all are notorious for fading the ball when they had to hit the fairway.
—COREY PAVIN

The Fade

A FADE IS A SHOT WHERE THE BALL FLIES intentionally from left to right. It is the well-behaved cousin to the slice, which also moves from left to right but with significantly more curving.

Arnold Palmer hit such a shot when he needed to reach the 18th green in the final round of the 1968 PGA Championship. When Palmer stepped to the tee of Pecan Valley's 470-yard final hole, he trailed the leader, Julius Boros, by a stroke. He hooked his thunderous drive into the rough, leaving his ball 230 yards from the green. To catch Boros, he needed to fade a three-wood shot over a creek and hill and onto the green close enough to sink a putt for a birdie three. The shot was long, and the odds were longer: in the history of the hole, only 19 golfers had ever birdied. Still, Palmer had no choice, and lined up for the shot.

FADING THOUGHTS

Like Palmer, you'll want to learn how to control your fade shot so it doesn't become a slice. Many players already come across the ball too much, that is, they create a downswing path that travels severely from outside to inside the target line. This causes the ball to curve more sharply than desired. Some also release the club-face—that is, they close the toe at impact—thus creating what is termed a "double

A PROPER PIVOT

Making a full shoulder turn is one of the most misunderstood concepts among weekend golfers. Two common mistakes come to mind immediately. Many golfers move their hips and shoulders as a unit. They shouldn't. When the hips and shoulders turn together, there's no foundation for the transfer of weight. The player who turns in this fashion typically ends up with a reverse weight shift, despite the fact that he or she executed a full shoulder turn. This ironic turn of events results from the hips turning with the shoulders, creating a kink in the forward knee. When you cut a notch in the trunk of a tree, the weight of the tree falls into the notch. Same goes in the golf swing.

A proper shoulder turn coils the weight into the inside of the back leg and behind the ball. The lower body is the foundation for the shoulder turn to coil the weight. In a proper turn, the shoulders start the turn, while initially the hips resist. Then, depending on the player's flexibility the hips turn to complete the backswing. The net result may be a 90-degree shoulder turn with only a 50-degree hip turn, leaving the player fully balanced and coiled into his or her back leg. A player with this position at the top of the swing will be able to unload or transfer weight powerfully back to the ball as the body uncoils from the backswing turn.

The other mistake occurs when golfers don't rotate their shoulders level to their spine angle versus level to the ground. Many golfers try to turn their shoulders too level because they've been told or are aware that they dip in the backswing.

Good players maintain their spine angle throughout the backswing by turning their shoulders level to their spine. To do this, maintain an athletic position, bending forward from the hips and flexing the legs at the knees. At the top, however, the left shoulder should be lower than the right because the spine angle is tilted toward the ground.

To feel a proper shoulder turn on the correct axis, lay a club across your shoulders and tilt forward from the hips, toward the ball. Turn your shoulders back so that the shaft of the club is over your back foot. If you maintained your posture, you'll feel a loaded sensation on the inside of your back leg. From there, you should be able to unload powerfully through impact.

THE FADE

The key to hitting a controlled and powerful fade is to contact the ball from the inside with the clubface slightly open. Assume a stance that is aligned parallel to the start line of the ball's flight (#1). Aim the clubface toward the final target. Position the ball slightly forward of center (sternum of chest). When you swing, make a normal coil and weight transfer (#2, #3), which will allow you to contact the ball at impact from the inside (#4–#10)—the key to a powerful, controlled fade. In the downswing do not allow the toe to close or roll forward of the heel at impact.

cross," which is hitting the ball left while already aiming left. A double-cross is akin to the double whammy because you're usually so far out of play that you're also "out of the hole," that is, reduced to trying to save a bogey.

KEEP YOUR OPTIONS OPEN

The key to hitting a controlled and powerful fade is to contact the ball from the inside with the clubface slightly open. You can accomplish this by: (1) making the adjustments in the pre-shot routine and (2) replicating them when you step up to hit the ball. Rehearse the shot and then hit it with confidence.

Usually, a fade becomes a slice because the player lifts the club up too abruptly in an attempt to fade the ball with the swing arc instead of using a pre-shot positioning of the clubface. Here's how to adjust pre-shot:

1. Assume a stance that is aligned parallel to the start line of the ball's flight.

2. Aim the clubface toward the final target (take your grip after the clubface has been aligned).

3. Position the ball slightly forward of center (sternum of chest).

4. If you normally hit shots with a slight right-to-left movement you might also try weakening your grip slightly, that is, rotating both hands on the grip about one-half-inch counterclockwise.

When you swing, make a normal coil and weight transfer, which will allow you to contact the ball at impact from the inside. Remember to strike the ball to the inside. This is the key to a powerful, controlled fade. In the downswing, feel your left hand holding on to the club slightly while not allowing the toe to close or roll forward of the heel at impact.

And if you need any motivation to help you overcome your fear, remember Arnold Palmer. As Arnie's Army came to know and love, Palmer played to win. So there was no wavering when Palmer pulled a three-wood from his bag and ripped a low-riding fade that landed just short of the green, bounded forward striking the pin, and came to rest eight feet from the cup. His loyal band of fans gathered around the green erupted with cheers. Some still call it the single-most electrifying shot in Palmer's legendary career. (The shot that followed was, unfortunately, one of his most disappointing: Palmer's birdie putt slipped by the cup and Boros held on to win the championship. But nevermind that now. The fade was fantastic. And yours can be too.)

Note: Two simple ways to practice hitting the fade: (1) Swing at balls placed below your feet on a sidehill. (2) Swing half speed at balls you're trying to curve around an object. Use the same setup and swing keys as explained above.

 ····· THE FADE ··

Common Mistakes
- Coming across the ball, right-to-left, too much; this is due to lifting the club instead of coiling back and approaching the ball to the inside (of the target line)
- Releasing clubface at impact, creating a "double-cross" (aiming left and hitting it so it also flies to the left)

Stance and Setup
- Assume a stance that is aligned along the start line of the ball's flight
- Aim clubface toward ultimate target
- Position ball slightly forward in stance
- If your natural ball flight is a draw, weaken the grip slightly (move hands counterclockwise)

Pre-swing Thoughts
- Visualize the ball curving from left to right and landing at the final target
- Trust the pre-swing adjustments— no further manipulations needed

Swing
- In backswing coil behind ball, making a solid weight transfer to back leg
- Swing along line parallel to target line
- Maintain open face of club through impact

–No.–
24

The draw is a more effective method of hitting the golf ball. The tail end hook, which is not really a hook but a curl, almost always adds a good many yards to the drive, and it is, for me at any rate, far more satisfactory in playing a long boring iron shot to the green. Further, a familiarity with its use does more than anything else to overcome one of the most troublesome things in golf—a hard crosswind off the left side of the fairway.
—BOBBY JONES

The Draw

THE MOST COMMON ERROR in attempting this shot is failing to start the ball to the right of the target. Once you've established the proper setup and made the correct backswing, you can release the club through impact. This, in turn, will bring the ball back to the left. The key is to learn to swing the club from the inside on the downswing. Then trust that the ball will start to the right of the target.

WHAT IS THE PROPER SETUP?

In the setup the stance is closed, right foot pulled back and clubface set square to your primary target, that is, aimed at where you want the ball to end its flight. Position the ball back in your stance the same amount of distance that you pull your right (rear) foot back in your stance. You can adjust depending on how much you want to curve the ball. This will give you a better chance of catching the ball as your clubface is still moving along a path that is slightly inside the target line.

If your natural tendency is to fade the ball, (hit it from left to right) strengthen your grip, rotating both hands clockwise about one-half inch. A strong grip will look like this:

- Hands are rotated to the right so you can see two knuckles on your left at address

- The palm of the right hand is facing up a little more than normal (looking down, you can see the clubshaft and the ends of fingers wrapped around the grip)
- The V between your thumb and index finger points to the outside of your right shoulder

Experiment with the adjustment to a stronger grip. The more you move the right hand alongside the shaft (and not on the top), the more it will rotate over the left hand in the downswing and at impact, thus closing the clubface. A smaller adjustment might be the difference between hitting draws and hooks. If the adjustment is too great—that is, you create too strong a grip—your swing will yield duck hooks, or smothered hooks (short, low-diving shots that curve severely from right to left). Remember, a draw moves from right to left with a gentle curl. A hook veers immediately and severely from right to left from the point of contact. At times, the more severely curving hook is the shot you should try to create, like when you're making a recovery shot around a tree. But generally, the draw, which is better behaved, is the shot that you want in your bag.

1994 U.S. AMATEUR

On the 33rd hole of the 1994 U.S. Amateur final at the TPC at Sawgrass, Tiger Woods needed to hit a low-riding right-to-left eight-iron to recover from the trees on the left. He could have chipped out and tried to save par but he elected to go for the green, "to make something happen." Here's how he hit the shot.

1. Slightly wider stance than normal, ball positioned slightly back of center
2. Feet, hips, and shoulders squarely aligned, but to the right of the target
3. Low, slow takeaway along the line of the feet
4. Sweeping motion, not a steep approach

Tiger judges the amount of the hook or curve by how much he sets the toe in at address. He does not try to manipulate the clubhead with his hands through impact.

With flagstick on the top-right portion of the green, Tiger hit a shot that landed just over a cross-bunker and ran up onto the green. He two-putted for par to keep the match even. Two holes later he made birdie and took home the championship.

In the setup to hit a draw the stance is closed, right foot pulled back (#1) and clubface set square to your primary target, that is, aimed at where you want the ball to end its flight. Position the ball back in your stance the same amount of distance that you pull your right (rear) foot back in your stance. Because the right foot is drawn back slightly, you will approach impact from an inside path (#2 –#8). Swing along the line created by the stance and toward the point where you want the ball to start. Allow the club to release toward the target. Stay balanced through the finish (#9, #10).

STANCE SETS UP SWING PATH

Swing along the line created by the stance and toward the point where you want the ball to start. Because the right foot is drawn back slightly, you will approach impact from an inside path. This helps the clubface close naturally as you release through the ball. The hardest part for a player learning this shot is to swing inside-to-out. Most amateurs swing out-to-in, or over the top.

Here are a few things you can do to promote an in-to-out swing: Set up with great posture, keeping your spine angle straight as you tilt forward from the hips. Keep your chin up, which leaves room for the shoulders to turn level to the spine angle without dipping. During the swing, keep your head behind the ball and let the hands release through the impact area. Because of the strong grip (right hand more alongside the shaft, palm facing upward and more to the right) the hands during the through swing and at impact will rotate the clubface slightly closed, thus imparting a draw spin.

USE YOUR BASEBALL SWING

Hit balls above your feet because it helps you learn the arc of the draw. Stand taller when the balls are above your feet and turn your shoulders on a less tilted plane—this will keep the club on a shallower plane. When moving down from the top, feel that you are swinging to the right. The release of the clubface will get the ball moving back to the right.

Practice a baseball swing. Swing the club around your body at belt or thigh level. This will help you promote a level or horizontal rotation of the shoulders. This encourages a swing path that is in-to-out and a draw.

SHOT BRIEFS

THE DRAW

Common Mistakes
- Swinging too far to the inside in the backswing, forcing the down-swing to come from over-the-top (outside-to-inside the target line)
- Failing to start the ball to the right of the target

Stance and Setup
- Align the body in the direction you want to start the shot; pull the right foot back

- Aim the clubface at the final target
- Position the ball slightly back of center
  (an inch or two behind sternum)
- Adjust to slightly stronger grip if you play a natural fade

Pre-swing Thoughts
- Setup and swing will reduce loft of the club
- The amount you adjust your grip, stance, and clubface
  (toe in, or ahead of heel) will determine the amount of
  right-to-left ball movement and height of shot
- Start the ball along the line of your stance; trust your
  release of the clubhead to bring the ball back to the left

Swing
- Swing along the line of your body alignment
  (shoulders, hips, thighs, knees, feet)
- Approach ball with slight in-to-out path
- Release hands through hitting area and during impact
- Maintain tempo and make solid contact at impact

The assumption is that you have to hit the ball low to be a good bad-weather player. But that's not the secret to it. Sure, sometimes you have to keep it down when you're playing a shot to the green. What is most important is hitting the ball solidly. A lot of people playing in the wind will swing harder, try to hit the ball harder. Their timing gets off and they don't make good contact.
—BYRON NELSON

Knockdown Shot into the Wind

HEADWINDS CAN TURN A FAMILIAR SHOT, such as a three-wood off the tee or seven-iron from the fairway, into a tumultuous ordeal. Likewise, attempting an infrequently hit shot such as a knockdown shot into the wind—a low, boring shot that will give you carry and maybe a little roll—routes your ball along another somewhat less-traveled path toward the target. Wind, when it's up and howling, is the single-most difficult element to deal with on a golf course. It must be respected in order to preserve your score.

Many of the world's greatest golf courses are found in places where the elements have created vast, challenging landscape—locations such as the coasts of Scotland, England, Ireland, Florida, California, and the plains of Texas. Not surprisingly, they also feature wind. If asked to explain the rigors of Pebble Beach, host of four U.S. Opens, golfers would agree on the factor that contributes most to the course's toughness—the wind that swirls and sometimes blows in gale force off Carmel Bay. Pebble Beach's hole number 7, a short par 3 of approximately 125 yards that is usually reachable with a pitching wedge, demands laser-like five- or six-iron shots when the wind is up. Wind is an integral part of golf. If you can't adapt, you can't excel.

AGAINST THE WIND

So what are the challenges of playing into the wind? First the obvious: your ball flies far less. But wind also plays on your ball's spin, magnifying it. The force of the wind pushes at the side spin, accelerating its rate of speed. A soft fade can turn into an ugly slice, and a gentle draw into a runaway hook.

It also plays on the psyche. Golfers immediately think, "I'm really gonna have to crush this one." This leads to mistakes like grip tension and overswinging, both faults that lead to errant shots regardless of the strength of the wind.

The knockdown shot is designed to minimize the wind's influence. Its ball flight travels at a lower trajectory and stays true (straight). In addition, a shorter, more controlled swing brings more precision and accuracy.

SET IT UP TO KNOCK IT DOWN

The most frequent mistake golfers make hitting the knockdown shot lies in the setup. They know that they need to move the ball back slightly, but they immediately shift their weight onto the left side (or front leg) in the stance. If you put the weight on the left side in the setup, the tendency is to finish falling backward with the weight on your right side. This is often referred to as a "reverse pivot" and causes you to pull up and off your shot prematurely. You're about to hit two of golf's ugliest shots: (1) a "duff" if you hit it fat, or (2) a "worm burner" if you skull it thin. The key is to shift the weight on to your left side during the swing so you can "trap" the golf ball at contact. This means contacting the ball at the bottom of the swing arc, hands ahead of a slightly hooded clubface.

There are two ways to hit a knockdown shot: (1) The Pre-set, which is the traditional method; and (2) The Dynamic, which is a non-traditional method. I prefer

REASONS FOR USING A KNOCKDOWN SHOT

1. Holds a low trajectory that stays true (straight), even into a wind

2. More accurate and easier to control

3. When you're between clubs, you can take an extra club, keep the distance but increase your accuracy

> *Direction is always of first importance, and since an opposing wind magnifies errors in striking, it allows fewer liberties then could be taken at other times.*
>
> **—BOBBY JONES**

the Dynamic knockdown. To hit this shot correctly, first take your grip an inch or two down on the club. This allows you to stand closer to the golf ball. As you move closer to the ball, you will feel more "on top" of the shot, which will help you to trap the ball against the ground.

Standing closer to the ball also gives you a shorter and more controllable swing. It helps ensure the ball is struck at the bottom of the club's swing arc with a square clubface. This produces a solid hit that travels at a lower trajectory.

Narrow your stance a bit so it's easy to load and unload the weight from the right or rear leg while taking only a three-quarter swing. Players tend to widen their stance for stability when trying to hit this shot, but it inhibits the transfer of weight and coiling with a shorter backswing. With a wide stance, it's harder to coil far enough to load to the right side.

Play the ball in the center of your stance with mid-irons and slightly farther back with short irons. This allows you to produce a normal golf swing, coiling and uncoiling without leaning on the left side and trying to hit down on the ball. Move your hands slightly ahead of the ball so the clubface stays square at impact.

Now that you're in the proper setup to hit a knockdown shot, all that's left is to swing the club. Take a three-quarter backswing and strike the back of the ball with a sweeping blow. On the downswing, uncoil into your forward leg, trapping the ball at impact. Finish with an abbreviated follow-through, allowing the club to raise no higher than the top of your shoulders.

THE PRE-SET KNOCKDOWN SHOT

The Pre-set (traditional) style is a riskier way to hit this shot because it's easier to fall into a reverse pivot. However, if you want to stick with the traditional, start by playing the ball back in your stance and keeping the same stance width. Set your weight on your left leg and move your hands forward of the ball to de-loft the club.

From the backswing through impact, keep the weight on your left leg. This protects you from falling back onto your rear leg at impact (the reverse pivot). There is very little lower-body movement in the Pre-set method, which is why you'll generate less power. It's best to use this shot for knockdown shots of shorter distances.

NEWTON ON THE TEE

When a club comes in contact with a golf ball, it transfers two types of energy: linear (for distance) and rotational (for spin). Each hit generates a limited amount of energy, so if more energy goes to rotation, less is available for distance. Because backspin counteracts the ball's tendency to fall, however, it enables a ball to fly on a flatter trajectory and once the ball hits the ground, it will roll farther.

Players successful at golf have undoubtedly learned to make spin work for them. The first step in acquiring this skill is to understand how spin influences the flight of the ball; then a player can plan how to impart the appropriate spin.

When a ball is hit dead on, pure backspin is imparted. Up to 8,000 revolutions per minute (rpm) can be generated. The angled face of the club pinches against the ball and makes it rotate backward toward the club. For just a millisecond, the ball actually climbs up the face of the club. The grooves on the clubface help generate backspin because they increase the amount of friction between the ball and the club. Conversely, wet conditions decrease friction and thus reduce backspin. A headwind increases backspin; a tailwind decreases it. Softer-covered balls stay on the clubface microseconds longer than harder-covered balls and hence have a faster spin rate. A ball's rate of spin is also determined by the relationship between the ball's core and its cover. A ball having a harder core relative to its cover will spin faster.

Backspin makes a ball rise.

Rotational forces generated by backspin increase the amount of lift experienced by a golf ball. Therefore, if a ball with backspin has the same trajectory as one without backspin, it will stay in the air longer. For example, if both trajectories have a height of 65 feet, a ball with backspin will stay in the air for six seconds and the one without backspin for only four seconds. These two seconds can equate to as many as 30 yards on the course.

The knockdown shot minimizes the wind's influence by providing a lower and straighter trajectory. A shorter, controlled swing is key.

TAKE MORE THAN ENOUGH CLUB

Club selection also plays an important role in hitting the right shot. You must take at least two factors into consideration: (1) the force and direction of the wind and (2) the type of shot that will give you the greatest probability of the lowest score. You're hitting against the wind, and that itself will decrease the distance of your shot. Gripping down on the club, a three-quarter backswing and low follow-through will curtail your length facing a wind of 20 miles per hour. Thus, add two clubs so you can relax and swing with good tempo. Keep in mind that any sidespin applied to the ball on contact will be greatly enhanced when traveling into the wind. As the renowned golf instructor Davis Love, Jr. once told his son, "When it's breezy, swing it easy."

Remember, when hitting into the wind concentrate on your ball striking. Hit the ball with solid contact and your shot will tame the wind.

DOWNWIND APPROACH SHOT

When the wind is behind you, it serves to diminish the backspin on an approaching shot, thus allowing it to fly lower and roll farther after landing. Here are the adjustments you need to make to hit this shot.

1. Drop down a club—use a wedge where you'd normally hit a nine-iron, and so on. Figure gearing down one club for each 10 mph. Grip down on the club slightly.

2. Stand closer to the ball, narrow your stance and position the ball in the center of your stance.

3. Swing three-quarters back and finish all the way on your left side. Concentrate on tempo and solid contact.

Common Mistakes
- Reverse pivot or hitting off the back leg
- Coming over the shot
- Club selection

Stance and Setup
Dynamic
- Grip down on the club an inch or two
- Narrow your stance
- Stand closer to the ball
- Position the ball in the center of your stance

Pre-set
- Standard stance width
- Play the ball back in your stance
- Set 60% of your weight on your forward leg

Pre-swing Thoughts
- Take two extra clubs and swing easy
- Stay on the left side through impact

Swing
- Take a three-quarter backswing
- Trap the ball at impact
- Low follow-through no higher than shoulder line

When a ball sometimes gets stuck on the side of a hill, especially on a lot of modern courses with mounding, the ball can get way above your feet, as much as knee high. First thing, choke down because the hill is bringing the ball much closer to you. Think of the swing as a more horizontal swing, like a baseball swing. Move the ball back in your stance. This will help you catch the ball cleanly and lessen the hooking effect of the lie.
—AL GEIBERGER

Ball Above Your Feet

WHEN TOM LEHMAN CAME ALONGSIDE HIS BALL resting on the fairway of the 17th hole at Congressional Country Club in the final round of the 1997 U.S. Open, he was in a three-way dog fight with Ernie Els and Colin Montgomerie for the lead. Lehman had just fallen one shot off the pace at the 16th hole when his seven-iron missed the green and he failed to get up and down.

Water encircled the entire left side of the 17th green, a mere 30 feet from the pin. Hitting the right side of the undulating green, the safe play, would most likely yield par. Going right at the flag was the riskier play—there was little margin of error should his ball sail too far left—but could put him below par if he hit it right. Lehman was running out of holes and felt he had to make something happen. He chose to go for the flag and the birdie.

Lehman's ball rested on a sidehill lie above his feet. His natural and favorite ball flight is a gentle draw, and he knew that the lie would exacerbate that. Taking "dead aim," he moved his aiming point away from the center of the green and closer to the pin. His shot—hit solidly but overcooked—splashed down in the hazard and went to a watery grave, and with it went Lehman's chances for a first U.S. Open title.

DON'T FIGHT THE SLOPE

When you play a shot such as Tom Lehman did on Congressional's 17th, the club needs to swing more around your body on a flatter and less upright plane. To create this plane adjust your posture, stand slightly taller, and take the club back lower, thus creating a wider arc and less upright plane. In the downswing approach the ball with a shallower angle and at impact sweep along the sidehill of the slope. Keep the clubface moving down the target line past impact. If you take a normal or more upright swing when you work your right shoulder slightly under the shot in the through swing, you'll hit behind the ball, producing a chunked shot. Grip down on the club from one to two inches. The more severe the slope, the more you should grip down.

Consider selecting one club less than normal because the slightly closed lie of

When this shot is hit from a very severe sidehill lie the ball will curve lower and faster. Adjust for this by slightly opening the club at address and aim to the right.

your club will effectively decrease the loft of the club, causing the ball to fly lower (and roll farther) than normal and move to the left. (*Note:* You can adjust for this somewhat by slightly opening the club at address. This will minimize the curving to the left and add loft to the ball's flight.)

Align the club slightly to the right of the target on the line you want the ball to start. Position the ball in the middle or slightly back in your stance along a target line that is parallel to your alignment of your feet, knees, thighs, and chest. Set your weight in the middle of your stance.

Make a controlled sweeping swing around your body, almost like that of a baseball player. Concentrate on making solid contact and full follow-through. The ball flight will curve to the left. When hit from very severe sidehill lies the ball will curve lower and faster.

*With the ball
above one's feet, the natural
(and in this case correct) tendency
is to stand more erect than usual and
—depending on the severity of slope—to
choke down on the club. In my case, setting
my weight more toward my toes and making a
special effort to swing smoothly and compactly
helps me to retain my balance, with a mental
picture of sweeping the ball away cleanly,
rather than digging it out of the hillside.
Generally I will go with the tendency
of the ball to draw, and simply
aim accordingly at address.*

—JACK NICKLAUS

If you're playing a hilly course the architect is likely to challenge you not only to hit a ball above your feet but also to fly it to a blind target. Hitting blind certainly adds to the degree of difficulty when hitting a ball above your feet.

The keys to hitting this shot are (1) employing good visualization and (2) picking an intermediate target. Initially, you must see the actual shot in your mind's eye. Then, you must pick out an intermediate target along a line that intercepts at the point where the target line disappears over the horizon. Select a twig or leaf or divot, or a discoloration in the grass, almost any distinct mark that is along the target line. Start the ball over that mark. For example, at St. Andrews' infamous Road Hole, No. 17, British Open contestants hitting their blind tee shots aim for the letters "Ol" of the name, "Old Course hotel," on the facade of the hotel wing that must be carried to reach the fairway.

Common Mistakes
- Failing to stand taller at address
- Not aiming far enough to the right
- Failing to move the ball back a little in the stance (which diminishes the effect of the lie and reduces the right-to-left curving)

Stance and Setup
- Align clubface along a target line that is right of the target
- Square feet along line parallel to start line
- Grip down on the club
- Position ball in middle of stance

Pre-swing Thoughts
- Make solid contact and think "sweep"
- Stay balanced and keep up consistent tempo

Swing
- Swing around body
- Take three-quarter backswing and full follow-through

Playing a shot where the ball is lying lower than the feet is one of the harder shots in golf and it's easy to understand why. Beginning golfers find it easier to contact the ball if it's raised in the air on a tee, more difficult when it's on the ground. Now, in the ball-below-the-feet lie, it's actually lower than ground level. The tendency is for the ball to be topped, pushed or push-sliced.
—GARY WIREN

Ball Below Your Feet

THE KEY TO HITTING A BALL BELOW YOUR FEET is hitting the entire ball, dead on. This sounds pretty obvious, but you'd be amazed how many players are thrown off by a ball sitting a few extra centimeters below foot level. They come up and out of the swing and hit the top of the ball. Or they hit the ball to the right because they've failed to keep the club square through impact.

The lie itself promotes a left-to-right ball flight. The slope increases your spine tilt, which causes a more vertical swing path. This more upright, less around swing path contributes to cutting across the ball, which sends a ball that's already "flying right" farther on its way. In order to execute this shot properly, you need to make adjustments in the setup and swing.

POSTURE IS IMPERATIVE

Select more club to compensate for the slight left-to-right flight the lie will produce, and for the less-than-full swing you will take. Position the ball in the center of your stance, even with your sternum. Align and aim slightly to the left of the target. Square the clubface along the line you will start the ball. Set your feet along a line parallel to the line on which you will start the ball.

Tilt forward more from the hips. Flex your knees more to support the weight of the upper body. Stand closer to the ball. Feel the weight more on the heels. Widen your stance slightly. This will help you counter any loss of balance caused by the pitch of the slope.

The ball below your feet on a sidehill calls for a slight posture adjustment, but don't overcompensate. You still must maintain a stable position at address and during the swing. This means keeping the chin up and the upper body tilted forward from the hips.

Poor posture, such as slumping too far forward, flexing too much at the knees or burying your head in your shoulders, creates swing problems. When you don't tilt forward from the hips, the club will naturally swing on a plane that's too far behind the body and too flat. This forces you to move from the heels to the toes on the downswing, leading to a constant feeling of imbalance and instability. This makes it difficult to achieve consistent, solid impact. As a reaction to the instability, you try to keep your head down to contact the ball solidly. This creates poor posture, thus completing the vicious cycle of excess head movement during the swing.

In contrast, a player with proper posture (chin up, tilted forward from the hips) is able to swing the golf club naturally on-plane and in front of the body. When the club is in front of the body, a golfer can maintain better balance throughout the swing. The result is a stable and steady head position through impact. Steadiness, stability and balance—you need all of these to hit a ball hanging below your feet.

STAY DOWN, FINISH LOW

Stay on the downslope and make a few half swings, then three-quarter swings. Determine which length and speed of swing allows you to make a solid pass without losing balance. With this shot you need solid contact and complete balance throughout. A controlled, balanced swing will prevent you from pulling off the ball, thus topping it, or falling forward during the downswing and hitting the ball off the hosel.

Take the club back one-half or three-quarters. Maintain knee flex throughout the swing, thus keeping the radius of the swing constant. Stay in your posture throughout impact. Finish low. Let the extra club or two you've selected and solid contact carry the ball to the target—do not add any "hit" to the bottom of the swing. Solid contact—the result of a smooth swing at an even tempo—will provide the distance and direction.

Note: More advanced players have mastered other approaches to hitting this shot. One method is to close the clubface slightly, align square to the target rather than playing for a slight left-to-right curving, and swing three-quarters.

BALL BELOW YOUR FEET

Common Mistakes
- Failing to stay in the correct posture for making solid contact with the ball
- Failing to make sure the bottom of the swing covers the ball
- Not using enough club, overswinging and losing balance

Stance and Setup
- Tilt forward from the hips
- Add more knee flex
- Grip club at full length and take an extra club or two
- Stand closer to ball, position ball in center of stance
- Aim left and set feet parallel to target line (aimed left)

Before hitting this shot, stand on the down-slope and make a few half swings and three-quarter swings to determine which length and speed of swing will allow you to make a solid pass without losing balance.

Pre-swing Thoughts
- Stay in correct posture throughout swing
- Maintain balance and tempo
- Finish low

Swing
- Take one-half or three-quarter backswing and through swing
- Maintain knee flex and posture through impact
- Maintain smooth tempo—stay balanced

With either a downhill lie or uphill lie,
always play the ball nearer the higher foot.
—JACKIE BURKE, JR.

Downhill

JACK NICKLAUS FAITHFULLY PREACHES that confidence breeds success. If you believe in your ability and the shot you're hitting, you'll produce positive results more often than not. So what causes a lack of confidence? One major contributor is discomfort. If you don't feel comfortable at address, you're less likely to hit the desired shot.

Hitting a downhill is a perfect example. A downhill shot occurs when the ball is in a position that forces you to stand with your body leaning toward the target. As you stand to the ball, your rear foot is higher than your front foot. This is not a stance you're used to; your balance is altered, and it's difficult to sense how much coil and shift you should employ. Many golfers start past the ball (ball back in their stance) and then pull back to the ball in the swing. The result? They raise the swing arc and hit the ball thin.

COUNTERING THE GRAVITY EFFECT

You need to counter the effect gravity has on your stance. It tries to pull the center of your body downhill (or past the ball). Here's what I would do to combat it:

First, set the shaft perpendicular to the slope. Then stand to the handle (point the handle just left of your center). Make sure your shoulders are parallel to the slope.

In the setup and stance of the downhill shot, position your shoulders parallel to the slope and set slightly more weight on the inside of your back leg. Concentrate on leaving your weight there throughout the swing. Minimize your backswing (#1, #2) to maintain control over your weight shift. After you reach the top, swing down the slope through the impact area, or chase the ball down the slope (#3–#7). Stay balanced and finish low (#8–#10) so that you don't catch the top-half of the ball and skull the shot.

In an effort to not allow gravity to pull you past the ball at impact, set slightly more weight on the inside of your back leg and concentrate on leaving it there throughout the swing. It's also better to play a fade or a cut shot, which will aid in getting the ball in the air. Set the face of the club slightly open and aim a bit to the left. It's a good idea to minimize your backswing to maintain control over your weight shift, and stay balanced during the swing. Take a few practice swings to see how long of a swing you can take and still maintain control.

CHASE DOWN THE SLOPE

After you take the club back and reach the top, swing down the slope. I like to tell students, "Chase the ball down the slope." Finish low so that you don't catch the top-half of the ball and skull the shot.

The ball flight is low so expect the ball to run once it hits the ground. You may even want to take one less club. The additional loft will help get the ball in the air —the main challenge when hitting a downhill lie.

STAYING UP ON THE FLAT

When watching a professional golf event on television, you'll often hear commentators comment, "He's staying up on the flat." What does it mean when they say this? Well, they're talking about course management. Staying up on the flat means landing your ball in an area that is flat ground. Pro golfers sometimes lay up so they can hit their approach off flat ground and avoid hitting off a hilly lie. You should do the same. Here's an example:

Say you're playing a short par 4 of approximately 340 yards. The last 100 yards of the fairway slope downhill toward the green. If you pull out your driver and blast the ball 240 to 260 yards off the tee (and this is assuming you've hit it straight), you'll be 80 to 100 yards from the pin, but hitting off a downhill lie. Instead, you might hit a fairway wood or long iron that leaves 120 to 140 yards. Now you're farther from the pin, but hitting from a more comfortable lie, and a full shot.

When hitting those soft approach shots into the green, you want the most comfortable lie possible. Do yourself a favor. Stay up on the flat and knock the next one stiff.

Note: Practice this shot when you get the chance. It's the only way to feel comfortable hitting it during your round. Downhill lies are also great practice for players who have trouble moving past the golf ball in the swing. To hit it squarely, you have to maintain your balance and swing down the slope.

 DOWNHILL

Common Mistakes
- Setting the shoulders against the slope
- Taking too big of a swing and weight shift
- Finishing high and failing to swing down the slope

Stance and Setup
- Set the shaft perpendicular to the ground
- Set shoulders parallel to the slope
- Stand to the handle, setting a little more weight to the inside of your right leg
- Position ball slightly to the rear of the sternum
- Aim your body a bit to the left of the target with the clubface slightly open

Pre-swing Thoughts
- Imagine hitting a fade
- Take a swing that can maintain your balance

Swing
- Take a restricted (three-quarters) backswing
- Swing the club, chasing the ball down the slope
- Finish low to keep you from hitting the ball thin

An uphill lie looks easy, and most players like it, but it does bring about an astonishing number of topped shots. In almost every case, he will stay back on his right leg, and strike upward or across the ball from outside to in.
—BOBBY JONES

Uphill

SAND BUNKERS, TREE STANDS, AND WATER HAZARDS receive much of the attention when it comes to addressing tricky golf course lies. With all due respect to the catastrophe these lurking par-wreckers sometimes bring, I respectfully submit that there are other, more subtle course elements that cause just as many (and sometimes even more) problems. Strategic landscaping, such as mounds alongside fairways, and general course architecture, such as sloped fairways and elevated greens, often result in uneven lies that can be tricky if you don't know what you're doing.

When your ball is sitting on terrain that leans directly away from the target, you have an uphill lie. The uphill lie can be a tough shot because it affects the player's balance and ability to move through the ball at impact.

The uphill lie is very similar in one respect to the downhill lie. Both have gravity as a main concern. Your address position is going to feel awkward. The tendency is to hang or fall back during the swing on uphill lies. When this happens, you scoop the ball or hit a drastic hook. The ball will fly extremely high in the air and fall way short of your intended target.

Players also fear catching the ground with the clubface and altering their swing path. They try to catch the ball too clean (as if they're hitting off of hardpan), pull up and off the shot prematurely. The result is a skulled shot (or shot hit thin).

WATCH YOUR WEIGHT

The way to combat this is to get your weight into your left side. Do this by narrowing your stance and positioning the ball slightly forward of the sternum. Focus on setting your weight toward the left knee. This will help to distribute the weight evenly between both feet, a necessity for balance. Try to get your hips and shoulders parallel with the hill. This will give a more normal position at address and

KNOW THE CONDITIONS

A variety of conditions can affect your shot from an uphill lie. Take all factors into consideration before addressing the ball.

The degree of the slope: **A slope of eight degrees will add eight degrees to the effective loft at impact, the equivalent of two clubs.**

Wind in your face: **In most cases, you'll want to take an extra club when hitting from an uphill lie. Under these conditions though, take at least two extra clubs. This is a high-trajectory shot so the wind will hold the ball up and curtail its distance.**

Wind at your back: **A strong wind should carry the ball enough distance so you don't have to take the extra club. Use the club you would use if you were hitting off flat ground.**

Wind blowing right to left: **Aim even farther right of the target than normal for this shot. You'll pull the shot and the wind will increase the distance the ball flies to the left.**

Wind blowing left to right: **Aim at the target. The wind (if strong enough) should counter a pulled shot and push the ball directly to the target.**

Fluffy lie: **Be careful with this shot. The fact that the ball is sitting on a slope in a fluffy lie makes it very unstable. If you ground the club and the ball moves backward, you'll incur a one-stroke penalty. Treat this like a bunker shot. Don't ground the club at address.**

Flyer lie: **Use the club you would use if you were hitting off of flat ground. This shot will fly much farther due to a lack of spin. Ignore the rule that a shot from an uphill lie requires an extra club.**

Position the ball slightly forward of the sternum (#1). Set your weight toward the left knee, your hips and shoulders parallel with the hill. When you begin your backswing, keep your weight set more over the left knee (#2–#4). Make sure the knee remains flexed throughout the swing (#5–#8). Coil inward slightly to generate power, but don't allow the entirety of your weight to fall onto your rear leg. Remember, you're already behind the ball. There's no need for anything but making a centered turn. During the swing make the clubhead follow the contour of the slope, thus ensuring square contact. Finish with your weight moving forward or uphill (#9, #10).

make it easier to hit the ball solid. Most of all, remember to set the shaft perpendicular to the ground and stand to the handle.

When you begin your backswing, keep your weight set more over the left knee. Make sure the knee remains flexed throughout the swing. Flexibility in the knees supplies your legs with support in the downswing and allows you to hit through the ball. Coil inward slightly to generate power, but don't allow the entirety of your weight to fall onto your rear leg. You'll run the risk of falling back too far and hitting the ball thin. Remember, you're already behind the ball. There's no need for anything but a centered turn.

Aim your body and club to the right of your target. How far right you aim depends on the severity of the slope. The greater the slope, the greater amount you must aim to the right. Because your lower-body movement is restricted for this shot, your weight shift will likely lag behind a bit in the downswing. It's easy to over-release the clubhead. When this happens you will hook the ball to the left. Factor this in to your setup.

THINK TEMPO

Rhythm and tempo are also important to hitting this shot. Concern about reaching the target, which can appear farther away at its uphill position, may cause you to overpower the shot. You'll speed up your hands and cast the club out ahead of your lower body. Instead of just pulling the shot, you'll end up snap-hooking it. Stay smooth and tempo-conscious through the shot.

Through impact and into the follow-through, try to make the clubhead follow the contour of the slope. This will ensure square contact. Finish with your weight moving forward (uphill) rather than falling backward.

Because it's very easy to slide the clubface beneath the ball on an uphill lie, you'll probably hit your shot slightly higher. The degree of the slope will affect the height and arc of the shot. If you're on an eight-degree uphill slope you'll effectively add eight degrees of loft to the club. Your six-iron is now an eight-iron. Be prepared to take one to three more clubs to hit the ball the desired yardage. This will also make it easier to maintain a smooth tempo, and not overswing.

Common Mistakes

- Falling back and losing balance during the backswing
- Swinging the club too hard and hooking the ball
- Not taking enough club to reach the desired target

Stance and Setup

- Narrow your stance to reduce your coil and weight shift
- Position your weight with a flexed forward knee
- Position the ball slightly forward in your stance
- Aim your body and clubface to the right of the target

Pre-swing Thoughts

- Stay on top of the ball during the swing
- Minimize weight transfer in your backswing

Swing

- Swing the club along the contour of the slope
- Maintain tempo throughout the swing
- Extend through the ball; do not scoop it
- Finish with your momentum moving forward up the hill, not falling back

SECTION V

PULLING RABBITS

OUT OF A

HAT

Avoid "sucker" pins. My game plan for approach shots is never miss the green on the side the flag is on. It's usually too tough to recover. If the flag is on the right, close to a bad bunker, I'm satisfied with a shot anywhere on the left half of the green. I'm taking most of the risk out of the shot, and I'll still have a birdie putt. Try never to miss the green on the flag side. I'll wager you'll score better.
—TOM WATSON

Pitch from a Tight Lie to a Tucked Pin

EVERY SO OFTEN, you'll play a round of golf where everything is clicking. Your drives off the tee, long irons, short game, and putting stroke—they're all flourishing. You're saying to yourself, "So this is what 'the zone' feels like."

I've seen many golfers experience rounds like this, only to see one mental lapse cause it to fall apart. It wasn't due to a mechanical breakdown or sudden case of the yips. They blew up because they got greedy.

One shot in golf where greed can be a deadly factor is the pitch from a tight lie in the fairway to a tucked pin. A short pitch from a tight lie is a delicate shot, and to attempt to knock it right at a pin tucked into the edge of a green guarded by hazards is very risky.

USE LOCATION, DON'T ABUSE IT

Whether it is greed or ego, golfers don't acknowledge the hazards of hitting to a tight pin. Even the world's greatest golfers rarely attack a tight pin unless it's Sunday afternoon and they're trying to win the tournament. Always consider the risk versus reward before attacking a closely tucked pin. The mature player won't try a shot he can't successfully execute a majority of the time.

For argument's sake, let's say you're 50 yards out in the middle of the fairway with a tight lie, and the pin is positioned on the back-right side of the green. There are bunkers in front of the green on the right and left and mounds of deep rough behind the pin.

If the clubhead hits the ground a little early on your shot, you'll dump the shot in the right bunker. Now, you need to hit your sand shot close enough to the hole to have a chance at getting up and down. But you catch the ball thin and hit it too far. Now you're faced with hitting a chip out of the rough with virtually no green to work with. All of this could have been avoided if you'd hit the perfect shot or a less-than-perfect shot towards a more accepting area of the green.

When it's absolutely necessary to pitch from a tight lie in the fairway to a tight pin, give yourself some room for error. Pay attention to the pin, but be aware of where you can safely miss the shot. Think big (the green), not small (the pin). There is nothing wrong with a six-to-eight-foot par-saving putt versus a tap-in when faced with this situation. In fact, your execution will improve by discarding an element of the risk. You'll be more relaxed and confident hitting the shot.

NO BOUNCE IS GOOD BOUNCE

The key to hitting the shot is to keep the club from bouncing off the turf before contact so you don't hit it thin. With no room under the ball, it's easy to catch the ball thin and blade it. To combat this common error, use the most lofted club in your bag with the least amount of bounce. I suggest using an L-wedge, but if you don't have one in your bag, you can use a sand wedge but you will have to de-loft it to reduce the effect of the bounce. The result is that you will hit the ball lower than if you played it with a lob wedge.

Set the clubface square to the target and weaken your grip. A weaker grip keeps the clubface from closing at impact.

Grip down on the club and stand closer to the ball. Set the butt of the club even with the ball and stand to the handle. Your stance should be 10 to 12 inches wide.

Swing the club back on plane toward the ball, keeping the body passive and controlling the club mostly with the hands and arms. The length of your backswing should control how far the ball carries. The club should swing down toward the ball like a plane making a landing, in effect shallowing through impact and sliding under the ball. The palm of the backhand should stay toward the target as if you were tossing a ball underhanded. You don't want to roll the wrists over before or during contact when hitting this shot. This would result in loss of height and backspin. Finally, finish on your left side with a follow-through comparable to your backswing.

When hitting this shot, think big (green), not small (pin). Play the shot that gives you some room for error. Six to eight feet is good; you don't need a tap-in.

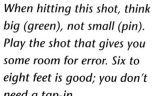

Weaken your grip slightly, that is, turn both hands counter-clockwise.

LESS CAN BE MORE

Take a "less is more" approach for this swing. Less effort ensures solid contact, greater control, and more consistency. Focus on rhythm and maintaining a smooth tempo through the shot. When you rush, the body typically outraces the arms and club, causing pushed, skulled, and even fat shots.

If you catch yourself aiming straight at a tight pin from this lie, step back and re-evaluate the situation. Don't fall victim to temptation. Ask yourself which shot you'd rather have for your next: a medium to short putt, or a short chip out of rough with two feet of green to work with. Know yourself and play the averages. If you can't honestly execute a shot eight of 10 times, you shouldn't be playing it.

Pitch from a Tight Lie to a Tucked Pin **159**

Golfers often allow their egos, or selective memory of a career shot, to control their decision-making. They remember the one shot they made and forget about the five shots they missed. They go for the tight pin, miss it to the short side of the green, and now face a delicate approach that must get up quickly and stop rolling almost immediately after landing.

This might be a good time to pull out the flop shot you've been working on. A flop shot is a very high, short shot that does not roll very far because of the extremely steep angle (created from maximum loft of the club) at which the ball hits the green. Here are a few things to remind yourself before execution.

- **The lie permits the shot.** You need enough of a grass cushion beneath the ball for the club to slide under; however, too much cushion and the club will slip under the ball without making contact.
- **Set the clubface open with the handle behind the ball, then center your body to the handle.**
- **When you stand to the handle the ball should be forward in your stance.**
- **Center your weight.**
- **Narrow and open your stance slightly.**
- **Take a full swing.** This may scare you because it's such a short distance to the pin, but the clubhead must move swiftly under the ball.
- **Keep the lower body quiet in the backswing.**
- **Keep the clubface open and sliding under the ball.**
- **Keep the club in front of the body in the downswing and finish on the left side.**

PITCH FROM A TIGHT LIE TO A TUCKED PIN

Common Mistakes
- Hitting straight at the pin
- Using a club with too much bounce off a tight lie
- Hitting off the back leg, trying to scoop the ball into the air

Stance and Setup
- Weaken your grip
- Narrow and open your stance slightly and stand to the handle
- Position the ball just forward of center
- Distribute weight evenly

Pre-swing Thoughts
- Be reasonable when choosing your target
- Think about tossing a ball underhanded
- Take the "less is more" approach

Swing
- Adjust your backswing to the distance of the shot
- Swing the club on plane toward the ball, keeping the club in front of your body
- Keep the loft of the clubface through impact, sliding the club under the ball
- Finish the shot with your weight on your left side

Everyday golfers aren't the only ones who find shots with less than a full swing difficult to execute. When you're trying to hit the ball a short distance, you have to remember that you control the length of the shot with the length of your backswing and follow-through. No matter what, you have to accelerate that club through the impact area.
—JEFF MAGGERT

Downhill Bump and Run to a Tight Pin Placement

THE MOST COMMON MISTAKE players make with this shot is allowing the club to swing up at impact. They end up catching the ball thin, skulling it, or they stub the club in the ground behind the ball. This delicate shot requires that you chase the club along the contour of the slope, thus contacting the ball high enough on the clubface to pop it slightly in the air. Should you take a shallow path that does not bottom out in the impact zone, the ball will strike the leading edge, what is term a "bladed" shot, or too low on the clubface to give it the gentle pop in the air that's needed.

Select your most lofted club, a lob or sand wedge. Address the ball with a slightly open and narrow stance. Position the ball directly off the right toe. The clubface is square to the target line and the butt end of the club is slightly forward of the right knee. Keep your shoulders parallel to the slope.

Just before swinging take two looks: The first glance is to the pin and the second is to your target. Remember, the grade of the slope is taking the ball down to the pin. You should be focused on landing the ball on the targeted spot, which will release the ball and let it roll down to the pin.

Hinge the club slightly in the backswing and drop the club-face down on the ball. Keep the club moving down the slope; and keep your hands in front of the clubface throughout the swing. Make a very short follow-through, no more than three or four inches. Your goal is to hit the ball into the fringe, or just onto the green, which will take the spin off the ball and allow it to roll toward the pin.

When I'm chipping, I do not like the ball to carry all the way to the flagstick. I want to get the ball on the ground quickly and let it run to the hole. On longer chips, if that means the best club to play the shot is a five-iron, then I'll use the five-iron. I frequently use my seven-iron and six-iron, as well. You shouldn't feel like some clubs are chipping clubs and others aren't.

—*JAY HAAS*

BUMP UP A HILL ONTO THE GREEN

Links-style courses often demand mastery of the uphill bump and run. When your approach misses the green and rolls down into a collection area, you need to bump it back up the hill and run it up close to the pin. Use this shot only when there is no flat spot—either on the green or just short of the green—on which to land your ball.

The exact spot of your first bounce is critical. You need to focus on this spot—usually one-half to three-quarters the way up the hill—and to land the ball where you're aiming. When this spot is properly judged and struck the resulting bounce will take the "juice" off the shot and feed the ball along the ground toward the target.

Select a six-, seven-, or eight-iron—whichever iron you are absolutely certain will not miss hitting into the side of the hill. Play the ball back in your stance, and stand closer. Make a short swing, bringing the club straight back and straight through, hinging the wrists slightly on the takeaway but keeping them firm through impact.

"GARDEN VARIETY" BUMP AND RUN SHOT

When you have an easy entry into a green—such as a flat surface, gentle slope devoid of any hazard—use a simple bump and run shot. By definition, this is any shot around the green deliberately played into a bank or slope to deaden the speed

Make a short swing, bringing the club straight back and straight through, hinging the wrists slightly on the takeaway but keeping them firm through impact.

while still allowing the ball to bound forward. Pick a club that will not put the ball in the air for any appreciable distance—usually a five- through eight-iron. You want the ball to land on the "bump" target and then run most of the way to final target. The greater the loft the more difficult it is to run the ball on the ground, and the more likely you will miss the "bump" target.

Address the ball with a slightly open stance, ball an inch or two back of center. Stand to the handle, butt end of the club directly in the middle of your body. Grip down on the club two or three inches using a putting grip. Edge closer to the ball.

Keep your weight slightly left by leaning the upper body toward the target.

Depending on the distance of the intended shot take the club straight back between 12 and 24 inches. On the through swing, strike down and through the ball. Finish with the weight on the left side and with the club low.

Practice this shot with several clubs and learn the carry and roll that each produces.

DOWNHILL BUMP AND RUN TO A TIGHT PIN PLACEMENT

Common Mistakes
- Reaching the point of impact with an ascending clubhead
- Failing to keep the hands ahead of the clubhead throughout the shot

Stance and Setup
- Place clubhead square to the target line
- Move the handle of the club forward
- Align feet in a slightly open and narrow stance
- Grip down on the club

Pre-swing Thoughts
- Look at ultimate target (pin) then look at landing target (fringe or edge of green)
- Let hands lead swing through impact

Swing
- Chase down the contour of the slope in impact zone and during follow-through
- Make a short follow-through and keep club low along the ground

Ask most golfers to hit a high pitch, and they flip the club upward through impact. Yes, this is one way to add loft, but few golfers can make this move without hitting chunks or skulls. The fact is, you rarely need more loft than what a squarely hit sand wedge provides. To hit it high, focus on swinging the clubhead long and low along the line on the follow-through.
—CRAIG SHANKLAND

Uphill Pitch to an Elevated Green

WHEN 48-YEAR-OLD JULIUS BOROS stood alongside his ball in the fairway just short of the elevated green of the 447-yard 18th hole of Pecan Valley in 1968 at the 50th PGA Championship, he knew that the ball of Arnold Palmer, who was only one shot behind, was resting eight feet from the pin. If Palmer made the eight-footer and Boros failed to get up and down, Palmer would take the championship in a dramatic two-shot swing.

Boros' short game was legendary, but now, in this pressure-packed situation, it would be put to the supreme test. Boros cracked a short pitch that flew nearly all the way back to the pin. It hit, bit, and held. He was four feet from the cup.

But he would have to wait to see if Palmer could make his putt. When Palmer missed, Boros knocked in his tester to save par. The victory was special—Boros became the oldest golfer, at 48 years and 4 months, ever to win a Major.

THREE PITCHING OPTIONS

The shots that separate good players from the field are those from 100 yards in, what is often termed the "scoring zone." Good players know how to score, and knowing how to score means knowing how to size up the shots that lead to low scores. Better players check not just the distance and the lie but also the pin position and the contour of the green. They consider what's between the ball and the intended landing area, the softness or firmness of the landing area, and the wind when determining what type of shot will produce the best chance of getting the ball close to the hole—to within the magic six feet where on average at least half of all putts are made. The pitch shot is often the shot of choice because it offers the widest range of options once the ball hits the green.

Heartaches usually begin when you're 50 to 75 yards out from the green. That is the valley of tears.

—*TONY LEMA*

1. You can fly the ball almost to the hole and have the ball bite.
2. You can fly the ball three-quarters of the way to the hole and have the ball run the rest of the way.
3. You can fly the ball one-third to one-half of the way to the hole and have the ball run the rest of the way.

And you can hit these shots with the pitching wedge, sand wedge, or lob wedge using the same basic techniques.

UPHILL LIE ADDS LOFT TO SHOT

The pitch shot taken from an uphill lie doesn't require extra loft in club selection. Because your ball is resting on an uphill slope you will naturally gain loft. For example, if your slope is 10 degrees and you're hitting a 60-degree wedge, you'll have 70 degrees of loft and an ample amount of trajectory. You won't have to open the clubface to increase trajectory.

To hit it, take a narrow, slightly open stance. Position the ball in the middle of the stance. Keep the weight over the left knee. This will help you to avoid falling backward. Square the clubface and grip down on the club. Take an abbreviated backswing and in the downswing strike the ball crisply. This will put spin on the ball and make it stop quickly.

COMMON MISTAKES

It's not uncommon to misalign the body and clubhead. When playing shots with an open or closed stance, it is sometimes difficult to keep the clubface square to the target. Often, when you open your stance you unconsciously aim the clubface to the left. The key to overcoming this is to aim the clubface at the target and then step into your setup.

Keep the face of the club looking skyward on the through swing.

Remember that you will naturally gain uphill loft on this shot because your ball is resting on an uphill slope.

Another mistake is not "standing to the handle," that is, the butt end of the club is not pointing toward the middle of your body. If your hands are too far ahead, such as opposite the front leg, chances are you'll hit low, solid shots or skulled shots by falling backward at impact.

SHOT BRIEFS ········· **UPHILL PITCH TO AN ELEVATED GREEN** ················

Common Mistakes
- Misaligning the body and clubhead. Aim the clubhead first, then step into your setup
- Allowing your hands to move too far forward at address, creating too much forward press

Strike the ball squarely. Do not manipulate the clubface through impact.

Stance and Setup
- Set the clubface square to the target
- Set the handle of the club even with the ball
- Stand to the handle with a narrow and slightly open stance
- Position ball opposite instep of front foot
- Grip down on the club
- Lean slightly into slope, keeping the weight just over the front leg

Pre-swing Thoughts
- No extra loft is needed—simply hit the shot leading with the front edge of the wedge
- Carry shot to the targeted landing area; do not allow for significant roll

Swing
- Match length of swing with length of shot: the shorter the shot, the shorter the swing; the longer the shot, the longer the follow-through
- Accelerate through at impact, striking the ball crisply
- Stay on the forward leg through impact

*Stopping the ball quickly from greenside rough is never
an easy shot, but I often play it just as I do a blast
from sand: Clubface open at address, abrupt or steep
backswing arc, contact about an inch behind the ball
while keeping my right hand well "under" my left.
Properly played, the ball will rise quickly and drop
softly. But again, don't try it without practice.*
—JACK NICKLAUS

Chip from
Heavy Rough
Just off the Green

ONE OF THE TRICKIEST SHOTS IN GOLF often happens after an almost perfect shot. Your ball lands on the green close to the pin but just kicks forward or to
the side in some heavy rough bordering the green. You've gone from the possibility
of birdie to the probability of bogey unless you know what to do.

When you have heavy rough surrounding the golf ball and you only want to hit
the ball a short distance, you need two main ingredients: (1) a steep angle of de-
scent and (2) a lot of loft. In order for the club not to get stuck in the grass before
impact, the club must come down on a steep angle. In order for the ball to be lifted
out of the grass, the club must strike the ball with enough loft.

The choice of club—you should use either a lob wedge or a sand wedge—depends
on how much green you have to work with once the ball lands, and your familiarity
with the individual ball flight patterns that these clubs produce for you. Knowing
how you hit with both clubs is crucial. If you've been practicing these shots, this is
where it pays off. Visualize the shot and where you must land the ball.

170

SMALL, PRECISE MOVEMENTS

Open the clubface slightly (approximately to one o'clock). After the clubface is set, take your grip. Set the shaft perpendicular to the ground and stand to the handle. (The butt of the club points just forward of your sternum.) Take a fairly narrow stance with about 10 inches of turf between your feet. Keep your weight centered.

Take a short backswing, hinging at the wrist. The arms move very little and the body stays quiet. Release the club back to the ball in a chopping motion. The shaft and the lead arm should end up in a straight line at impact. The club should finish very low and the body weight should be posted into the forward leg. The ball should pop out of the rough then land softly onto the green.

When you are very close to the green in deep rough it takes courage and commitment to swing firmly through a shot knowing that your intended landing spot is just a few feet away. After you decide how firmly or easily you must swing, you cannot let indecision creep into the shot at midswing. The result will be a poor shot.

Match in your mind and with a few practice swings the length of the backswing to the distance of the shot. Feel the rhythm of the swing. On the through swing, avoid "quitting" or decelerating or jabbing. Remember: have the courage to commit, and don't quit.

Rough is always tougher to get the club through when it is wet, so take extra pains to avoid it. When you do get in it, use a club with plenty of loft to get out.

—*JOE DANTE*

REHEARSE AND THEN HIT THE SHOT

Practice swings, or rehearsal swings, can help when executing a difficult shot or a shot that requires a heightened sense of feel. Most tour pros make a few practice swings when preparing to hit a pitch or chip. These rehearsals serve to relieve tension, help the player to visualize the ball flight of shot, and reinforce in the mind's eye the pace and length of the swing.

So go ahead and make a few practice swings. Then duplicate the rehearsal swing when you step up to the ball. To paraphrase Mark Twain, the results will pleasantly surprise you and astonish your playing partners.

Take a short backswing, hinging at the wrists. Release the club back to the ball in a chopping motion, keeping the clubface square through impact.

SHOT BRIEFS

CHIP FROM HEAVY ROUGH JUST OFF THE GREEN

Common Mistakes
- Ball too far back in the stance
- Too much arm swing or body movement
- Moving forward of the ball at impact

Stance and Swing
- Open the face slightly, then grip the club
- Set the shaft perpendicular to the ground
- Stand to the handle with weight centered

Pre-swing Thoughts
● Keep body and arms passive and mainly use wrists
● Imagine making a swing that looks like a checkmark

Swing
● Hinge the club up abruptly using the wrists
● Release the club down to the ball, holding the face open through impact

Just like on a full shot, your hips must turn through impact, except to an abbreviated finish. Most amateurs get too handsy, which limits ability to control loft and distance.
—TIGER WOODS

Less-Than-Full Wedge Shot

IT'S AXIOMATIC THAT WHEN ON THE GREEN, the closer you are to the hole the better off you are. However, when it comes to hitting your approach shot, proximity to the hole can have its special set of problems. I guarantee most golfers would choose to hit a 135-yard approach shot over a 65-yard shot: From 115 yards, you can hit a full wedge shot. Standing 65 yards out from the pin you can't take a full swing. These half and three-quarter shots give golfers high blood pressure.

FEEL IS TOUGH TO LEARN

Less-than-full wedge shots require feel—the ability to sense and control clubhead speed and ball flight. To develop feel you need the correct technique and lots of practice. The greatest mistake amateur golfers make is they decelerate their hands during the downswing in fear of hitting the ball too far (or too hard). Their weight falls backward while the club lags behind. The result is a chunked shot that travels only a few yards or a skulled shot that careens across the green. Now instead of a 65-yard shot to set up a birdie putt, you're recovering in order to get close enough to save par.

The second problem is that golfers are unaware of the distances they hit the sand wedge, pitching wedge, and lob wedge. If you don't commit these distances to memory, you won't know which club to hit and how to swing it.

Do your homework. Know the distances you carry for each club. For example, I carry a pitching wedge 115 to 120 yards, a full sand wedge 95 to 100 yards and a full lob wedge 75 to 80 yards. I also know the distances I hit these clubs after slight alterations. For example if I grip down on a pitching wedge and take a swing of three-quarters or less, I hit it 90 to 100 yards (which overlaps the distance that I hit my full sand wedge).

As a beginner, I spent twice as much time practicing my short game as I did beating balls with my driver and fairway woods. This really had a positive impact on my overall play. Most of your shots on the course are from 100 yards in, so why wouldn't you want to be good at those things you do most often?

—JIM FURYK

The fact that I can hit two different clubs—pitching wedge and sand wedge—between 90 and 95 yards allows me to consider the conditions and select from the two. For example, let's say I'm 95 yards from the pin. If I'm coming into a big green that pitches steeply forward and the pin is set all the way toward the back, I don't want to hit a sand wedge with a lot of spin. It might land at 95 yards, but then suck back three to five yards because of the spin on the shot and contour of the green. Instead, I would take a pitching wedge, which has a lower ball flight and not as much spin. It may land 90 yards from the pin, but then release and run back to the pin. So even though I carry both clubs a difference of five yards, the result (once the ball comes to rest on the green) could be as much as 10 yards.

Most important, I know these distances because I have practiced these shots. You cannot expect to be precise with your feel on the course if you haven't spent time practicing on the range.

PLAYING THE SHOT

When playing a shot that requires less than a full swing of any of the three wedges, narrow the width of your stance and position the ball in the center. By narrowing your stance you will be able to coil onto your back leg even with a short

Grip down slightly on the handle.

The number one mistake that golfers make on this shot is decelerating and hitting the shot off the back leg.

backswing, and therefore uncoil through impact onto your forward leg. This ensures solid, crisp contact. The number one mistake that golfers make on this shot is decelerating and hitting the shot off the back leg. The result is either a fat or skulled shot.

Next, grip down on the club one-half inch for every quarter you are shortening your swing. For example, grip down one inch for a half shot. By gripping down on the club you will narrow your swing arc, in effect reducing your clubhead speed. It will also naturally straighten the path of the swing, thus increasing your directional control.

By practicing these adjustments with all three wedges (PW, SW, LW) you will be able to develop a predictable arsenal of shots from 30 to 100 yards. For example, if your normal sand wedge goes 100 yards, your three-quarter sand wedge will go 75 yards, while your one-half sand wedge will go 50 yards. The distances of your wedges will overlap but the trajectories will be different. Your one-half pitching wedge will go the same distance that your three-quarter sand wedge will go except it will fly lower and will roll farther.

On the course when faced with a 60-yard shot into a strong wind with a lot of green you would be able to confidently hit a one-half pitching wedge to your target. On the next hole you may be faced with a 75-yard slight downwind shot to a pin with less green to work with. There you would choose a three-quarter sand wedge

or even possibly a full lob wedge. You can see the possibilities. If you practice these shots you will have confidence to execute them on the course.

SHOT BRIEFS · · · LESS-THAN-FULL WEDGE SHOT ·

Common Mistakes
- Too much club, too wide of a stance, too big of a backswing
- Deceleration during the forward swing
- Not enough knowledge of club distance
- Not enough practice to learn distances

Stance and Setup
- Grip down on the club one-half inch for every quarter you shorten the swing
- Narrow your stance to match your backswing length (1/2 backswing = 1/2 stance)
- Play the ball in the center of your stance

HAVE A PURPOSE FOR EACH SHOT

Yes, half and three-quarter wedges are among the toughest shots in golf, but they can sometimes be avoided through intelligent course management. Before hitting a shot from the fairway (or rough), always think ahead to the next shot. Have an idea of how far you want to hit the next shot before pulling a club out of your bag.

Let's walk through a par-5, 500-yard hole. You hit a nice drive into the fairway that carries and rolls about 240 yards. You are in the fairway and have a clear look at the green, but still have another 260 yards to travel. The object here is not to cover as much distance as possible with your second shot. Think ahead to your third shot. What short-iron is most comfortable in your hands? Are you better when faced with a 115-yard pitching wedge than a 55-yard shot? If so, then hit your next shot 145 yards to a spot in the fairway that will give you a good angle to attack the pin. Take out your seven- or eight-iron and lay up. This makes more sense than blasting your five-wood and being faced with a 55-yard half-wedge over a bunker.

A smart golfer is a better golfer. Course architects are rarely hired to build driving ranges.

Pre-swing Thoughts
- Shorten the backswing enough to be able to smoothly accelerate through the ball
- After you have made your choice, commit to the shot

Swing
- Match backswing length to distance of shot
- Coil and uncoil weight despite the length of shot
- Smooth acceleration through impact
- Finish on forward leg facing target

*If I want a lot of height on a fullish pitch shot,
I break or cock my wrists quickly on the backswing, then use them very actively to "throw"
the club under—not down on—the ball. Properly
executed, this flips the ball high.*

—JACK NICKLAUS

Super Lob to a Tight Pin on an Elevated Green

A LOB SHOT IS ONE THAT YOU PLAY HIGH into the air with the intention of carrying it a short distance and stopping it almost immediately after landing. When faced with an elevated green and a pin placement very close to where the ball will enter the green you must add a lot more height to the shot. Thus, the super lob.

Tiger Woods faced this difficult shot on the 10th hole in the final round of the 1999 Western Open. As he made the turn he held a slim lead. His approach at the 10th sailed over the green, leaving him approximately 15 yards over a bunker to the pin, which was situated close to the front edge of the green.

This shot is hell for most golfers, even the very best. There is a lot that can go wrong. Golfers who play without an L-wedge (lob wedge), a wedge with a loft of 58-degrees loft or more, and thus hit this shot by opening the face of a sand wedge, often end up with a skulled shot. This is caused by the back edge of the club bouncing as it makes contact with the turf, which in turn causes the leading edge of the clubface to strike the ball. Others move laterally during the downswing, and then pull back on impact, producing skulled shots that fly fast and low, usually

Hit this shot with the grip of the bottom (left) hand slightly weakened, stance slightly open, your hands at address set even or slightly behind the position of the ball.

coming to rest somewhere over the back of the green. Just when you need a precision shot—as Ken Venturi would say, a shot that resembles "a butterfly with sore feet landing on the green"—you've launched a rocket that's overshot its landing zone.

GO SKYWARD

Here's how to hit what I would call a super lob shot, that is, one that features a short distance to the target but extraordinary elevation and a short roll-out to its stopping point. Set the club behind the ball, and then pull the handle and shaft back approximately an inch behind the ball. You should see the face of the club more toward the sky. This adds loft.

Weaken the left hand in the grip and stand to the handle, that is, take your stance with the butt end of the shaft in the middle of your torso or along an imaginary line that passes up through the sternum and center of the body. This should give you a slightly open stance with the handle in the center of your body. Your hands will be set at address even or slightly behind the position of the ball.

Take a narrow stance and position the ball slightly forward of the middle of the feet.

Next, take the club back along the stance line (imaginary line formed by your shoe tips) and allow the wrists to break early, thus creating a steeper backswing. Keep the right elbow close to your right side but in front of your body.

Swing the club down in front of the body, sliding the club under the ball through impact. Allow the body to move with club through impact, finishing with the weight posted on the forward leg. The ball should rise quickly as it rides up the club-face straight up into the air, float gently toward the target and land very softly.

You should consider using this shot when very close to the green, perhaps five to 20 yards from the targeted landing spot.

Standing just 15 yards from the pin, Tiger Woods knew what he had to do if he wanted to keep his lead. He hit a floating shot with a very high trajectory that carried over the bunker and landed short of the pin. It rolled forward and stopped close enough to the cup for a tap-in par. This par-saving shot helped him go on to win the tournament.

WATSON RIDES DEVILISH SHOT TO U.S. OPEN CHAMPIONSHIP

In the final round of the 1982 U.S. Open played at Pebble Beach Golf Links, Tom Watson played a devilish approach shot closely akin (in execution and ball action) to the lob to forge a lead that he took to the victory stand. When Watson came to the tee of the 17th hole, he and Jack Nicklaus were tied (Nicklaus had just finished playing the 18th). The 209-yard, par-3 17th hole is extremely wide but narrow from front to back. It is guarded by bunkers in the front and the ocean in the back. Watson's tee shot stopped in ankle-deep rough, pin high, but a treacherous 10 feet from the flagstick.

In the execution of the shot Watson used many of the same techniques used in the lob shot. He opened his setup and clubface, then took the club up abruptly on the backswing by hinging the right hand sooner. This helped him avoid catching the club in the grass on the takeaway. On the forward swing Watson slid the clubhead under the ball, holding with the club's face firmly open. According to Watson, when using this swing path he can "even hit slightly behind the ball, as if I were in the sand, with good results."

Watson's shot rose three feet and landed on the edge of the green. The ball rolled gently down the slope and into the cup for a birdie two —and the lead. Watson, needing only par on the 548-yard 18th to win the tournament, nevertheless birdied it from 20 feet.

SHOT BRIEFS

SUPER LOB TO A TIGHT PIN ON AN ELEVATED GREEN

Common Mistakes
- Trying to lift or scoop the ball into the air
- Bouncing the sole of the club off turf behind ball
- Moving laterally, sliding ahead of the ball
- Pulling back, hitting off the back leg

Stance and Setup
- Narrow stance and position ball slightly forward of middle
- Set club behind ball and pull handle one inch behind the ball
- Weaken grip with left hand (turn clockwise)
- Stand to the handle
- Set hands slightly behind ball

Pre-swing Thoughts
- Think about sliding club underneath ball
- Use shot when close to pin, five to 20 yards' distance, and when less risky alternative shots leave little chance for getting up and down in two strokes

Swing
- Take club back along stance line (formed by tips of shoes)
- Break wrists early
- Create a steep backswing

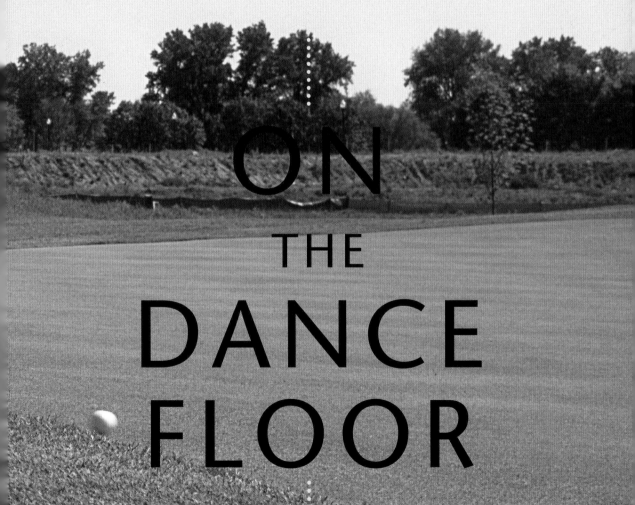

SECTION
VI

ON
THE
DANCE
FLOOR

By the time I was seven my golf was proficient enough for me to play with the caddies, who had to be over 14 by law and many of whom were pretty handy players. Of course, I was outgunned by the boys twice my age, but that may have been a blessing in disguise. I formed the firm belief that if I could get the ball onto the green, even near the green, I had a chance because I could compete against anybody once the time came to get down to putting.
—ARNOLD PALMER

Ball Resting against the First Cut of Rough Just off the Green

I'D EXPECT TO FIND THIS DICEY SHOT—putting a ball resting against the first cut of rough—in the bag of a gritty competitor such as youthful, overachieving Arnold Palmer, just as it found its way into Tiger Woods' bag as a junior player. It is part improvisation, part standard procedure, and all "can do," the attitude of great players that allows them to somehow get the ball in the hole from almost anywhere. The shot can be hit two ways, using a putter or a three- or four-fairway wood. Tiger Woods has demonstrated success by hitting the shot with his three-wood. It works for Tiger, and it can work for you.

Just remember when choosing a wood to putt a ball resting against the first cut of rough just off the green that the lie angle of the wood is designed for a circular swing, which forces you to stand much farther away from the ball. Make two adjustments. First, grip down on the handle. Next, raise the heel of the wood until its shaft angle parallels that of your putter. This will allow you to stand closer to the ball—and thus produce a more linear, putting-like stroke. At first this may seem awkward—you'll feel crowded. Stick with it—you'll soon be saving par with regularity.

USING THE PUTTER

The mistake that most players make with this shot is that when they make their stroke they catch the grass before contacting the ball. The result is poor contact, which prevents them from predicting how far the ball will roll. The key to any good putt is solid contact; a putt with the ball against the fringe is no different. You must ensure solid contact. Here's how.

> *The reality of the game of putting is that not all well-struck putts go in, and that sometimes poorly struck ones do. Statistically speaking, your chances of making any given putt improve with the quality of your putting skills. But your odds of success will never be anywhere near 100 percent, even if you are perfect in every stroke you make.*
>
> **—DAVE PELZ**

First, set the club behind the ball and de-loft the clubface by moving the handle toward the target. Practice moving the clubface backward so it sweeps up and above the blades of grass. Sweep it forward in a slightly descending arc, making sure that it comes back down squarely, contacting the ball before the grass.

Next, stand to the handle. By this I mean position your body so that the butt end of the putter is aligned opposite the midline of your body. This should position the ball and clubface on the target line just in front of your rear foot. Remember that the butt end of the putter should be positioned in the middle of your body and the ball should be positioned toward the rear foot. This is crucial if you are to clip the top of the grass and not stub the club during the through stroke.

Now, make a rhythmic stroke, keeping the wrists firm. Do not flip the putter face —keep it slightly de-lofted throughout the stroke. The ball will pop up slightly when you strike it. Then it will roll forward, picking up speed from the overspin created by the descending blow.

A reminder: do not make a conscious hit when striking the ball. You want the hands and wrists to remain firmly in control of the clubface, but you don't want to add any force from a pronounced wrist break or slap with the right hand.

Do not make a conscious "hit" when striking the ball—keep your stroke smooth through impact.

USING THE FAIRWAY WOOD

This variation is a very useful shot to have in your bag, and it can be mastered with a little bit of repetition. A fairway three- or four-wood is often a good choice because it more easily displaces grass, preventing the clubface from getting stuck or caught. The sole plate allows the club to glide through grass and the angle of the face provides just enough loft to get the ball up and rolling.

You should consider using this shot when you have a longer distance to the cup—say, at least 20 feet. The increased mass of the wood will enable you to stroke the ball more easily.

SWEEP, DON'T HIT

Here is how to master this shot. Set the club square to the target with your hands slightly forward of the ball position. Grip the club all the way down, almost touching the metal part of the shaft. You can use a normal grip or a putting grip—experiment and choose whichever feels more comfortable.

Position the ball slightly forward of the toe of your rear foot, just as you would in hitting a short chip. Take the club back low along the top of the grass and sweep into the back of the ball. Do not "hit" the ball. Keep the hands slightly ahead of the clubface throughout the stroke. The ball will pop up in the air slightly and then roll.

BALL RESTING AGAINST THE FIRST CUT OF ROUGH JUST OFF THE GREEN

Common Mistakes
- Catching the blades of grass before contacting the ball
- Positioning butt end of club too far forward of body's midpoint

Stance and Setup
Putter
- Set the club behind ball and de-loft clubface
- Stand to the handle

Fairway Wood
- Stand tall and place hands slightly ahead of ball position
- Grip down on shaft
- Position ball slightly forward of the toe of right foot

Pre-stroke Thoughts
Putter
- Concentrate on line—think, "I can make this putt." Don't just try to get it close
- Allow for overspin to roll ball toward hole
- Think, "Stroke the ball," not "Hit the ball"

Fairway Wood
- Consider using when distances are greater than 20 feet
- Allow for loft of wood to bump into air
- Think of sweeping into back of ball, not "hitting" ball

Stroke
Putter
- Keep body still throughout backswing
- Keep clubface de-lofted through impact
- Make a descending path to the ball

Fairway Wood
- Keep body still throughout backswing
- Sweep club along target line
- Keep hands slightly ahead of clubface

In most greenside situations, my goal is to get the ball rolling like a putt as soon as possible. I figure I have a better chance of judging and ultimately holding this type of shot than I would if I were to try to loft and spin the ball.
—GREG NORMAN

Just off the Green— To Putt or Not to Putt

IRREGULAR SHOTS ARISE WITH REGULARITY on the golf course. They come in a wide variety. Some are nearly impossible to execute, such as a ball resting between two tree roots. Others are merely difficult but lend themselves to an imaginative solution, such as rebounding a ball off a tree or wall when your normal swing is obstructed. Others, not so exotic, offer a more conventional low-risk, high-reward proposition. For example, when playing a ball just off the green on the fairway, you must choose (1) to putt or (2) not to putt. Ultimately, it's a matter of condition and comfort. Are you a confident chipper or pitcher? Is putting your forte? How challenging are your lie and the surrounding turf? Answer those, and you'll know what to do.

CHECKING THE GRAIN

For most golfers, putting is the safe call, lowering the risk of a drastically missed shot. Nothing catastrophic will happen if you hit a controlled shot on the ground, especially if the ball is rolling with the grain. Using a putter from off the green when the grain on the fringe is running against the shot, however, is a common mistake.

Putting into the grain of just a few feet of fringe makes distance and direction difficult to control.

Amateur golfers often dismiss the idea of using a mid-iron or short-iron from just off the green because they harbor images of a skulled shot racing across the green or a chili-dip that travels a foot or two. From a tight lie, there is no cushion of grass beneath the ball. The ball striking must be precise. I'm sure, however, that if golfers practiced bumping the ball onto the green when against the grain, they'd develop greater confidence addressing the ball with an iron than they would with a putter.

To check the grain, first ask yourself, "How are the blades of grass lying?" Check the sheen (brightness) of the surface. If it's down grain, it will look shinier when looking toward the target. When it's into the grain, it looks darker or duller.

The location of the drainage helps determine the direction of the grain as well. When water drains toward the low end of the green, grass will generally grow in the direction the water is draining. As I mentioned, if the grain is growing with the direction of the shot, I'd use the putter. When I'm against the grain, depending on the distance, I'd use an eight- or six-iron with a putting stroke. The loft of the iron elevates the ball just enough to get it over the grainy fringe and onto the green and rolling.

THE BUMP AND RUN SHOT

When the grain is growing against the direction of the shot we use the bump and run shot. Because the ball takes to the air for a short distance (a few feet), it skips over the grain and takes its influence out of the shot. Use the odd- or even-numbered clubs in your bag when practicing the bump and run shot (9-7-5 or PW-8-6). Don't spend time getting used to every club for this shot because the difference in loft is not significant enough from one club to the next.

To hit a bump and run shot correctly, focus on the set up. The actual stroke is nearly the same as your putting stroke. To start, align your clubface to the target. Set the shaft upright and stand the club on its toe end. This means that you address the ball with the lead edge flush to the ground, and then pick the heel up off the ground. Employing just the toe of the club reduces any drag that's created from the heel or sole brushing the ground.

It also sets the shaft more upright similar to the lie angle of the putter. This naturally helps the club to swing on a straighter more precise line with a one-level motion—that is, no wrists are used.

Next, move the handle forward slightly to de-loft the club. This will put overspin on the ball when it's contacted. When taking your stance, align the center of the body to the handle (stand to the handle, which means to align the butt end of the

ACKNOWLEDGE THE CONDITIONS

There are a few other elements to consider when faced with a shot from just off the green in the fairway. There may be an uphill or downhill slope to the green. The surface leading up to the green may not be smooth or could be wet. These conditions must be factored in to your decision making.

Slope: It's generally best to bump the ball with an iron uphill and putt when the slope runs downhill. Use an iron that has a little less loft (such as a five- or six-iron) when chipping uphill so the ball has more overspin and runs up the hill. Use a putter when hitting downhill to the green because it's easier to control distance. A short chip will have topspin, and may roll too far past the hole.

Rough or wet conditions: These are best contested with a more lofted iron. Whenever possible, you want to carry or skip over an unpredictable surface. It will help you to control the distance and direction of your shot. An eight-iron, nine-iron, or pitching wedge cannot "get stuck" in the wet turf if it carries over it. So if you choose to hit over wet conditions, pick a club that will lift the ball quickly out of the wet grass safely onto the green. If you choose to skip a ball through wet turf, use a less lofted iron. Its trajectory is shallower, which will help to keep it moving along the top of the surface.

handle at the midsection of your body). At this point the ball should be aligned even with the instep of the back foot. Again, the shaft is nearly vertical for this shot, which enables you to swing the club on a straighter line. When you take your grip you may use your putting grip or your normal grip. However, if you use your normal grip, shift the shaft more into the palms versus the fingers.

USING MORE OF THE TOE OF THE CLUB

According to Nick Faldo—the first player to win back-to-back Masters (1989 and 1990) since Jack Nicklaus did it in 1965 and 1966—chipping with the club up on its toe gives you options. "Players set the club on its toe for chipping for various reasons. If the ball is sitting down a little, it brings less of the club into contact with the ground. Or sometimes, if you are chipping onto a downslope on a very, very fast green, the ball will come out a little bit 'dead' if you set the club on its toe—it doesn't come out with the full spring of the club. Some guys just like doing it because they get their hands up high and just use a putting stroke, removing any other mechanics from the stroke."

Your upper body should lean slightly toward the target. You should feel a little more of your weight on your forward leg. If you've set the club properly, your hands should be ahead of the ball. This will help you trap and catch the ball solidly.

All that is left is to hit the ball, and that is accomplished by using your putting stroke. Finish with clubhead low with a slight transfer of weight to the left side.

Keep your legs still, and take the club straight back using your arms and shoulders. The proper stroke is the same length back as it is through the ball. Maintain an even tempo and keep your head still. The ball will lift into the air a few feet, land softly, and then roll forward due to the overspin. The greater the distance to the pin, the greater your backswing—just like your putting stroke.

Make a conscious effort to keep your hands moving forward toward the target following contact. To accomplish this, point the clubhead at the target in your follow-through. Quitting—stopping the hands once the ball has been struck—is a

Square face to target.   *Stand the club up.*   *Move handle forward.*

common mistake and will leave the ball short of your intended target. Keep the wrists quiet and the hands moving toward the target.

USING YOUR PUTTER

As mentioned, when you're hitting with the grain, it's okay to use your putter. Take your normal stance and simply lengthen your backstroke. Maintain smooth acceleration through the ball and keep your head down. Picking your head up to catch a glimpse of your shot may raise the lowpoint of your swing and cause you to hit the top of the ball.

Estimating the distance of longer putts greatly relies on trusting your judgment. When a friend at home asks you to toss him a set of keys, your brain calculates the distance and sends the message to your body to throw the estimated distance. Take that same approach when hitting long putts. Trust your instinct.

Greater distances make judging direction more difficult as well. Find an intermediate target along your line to help direct your putt. Your target may be a burned-out spot on the green, a spike mark, or some sort of discoloration. Find an intermediate target and then focus on the distance to the hole.

Stand to the handle.   *Make a putting stroke.*   *Finish low and left.*

Remember, the toughest aspect of this shot is club selection. Study the surrounding elements and execute the shot that makes sense. Once you've made the correct decision, you are more than halfway home. Now you just have to knock it close, or even make it.

SHOT BRIEFS

JUST OFF THE GREEN— TO PUTT OR NOT TO PUTT

Common Mistakes
- Putting against the grain
- Chipping with the grain
- Picking the head up early to see the shot
- Quitting after contact

Stance and Setup
Bump and Run
- Align clubface to the target
- Set the shaft upright and stand the club on its toe end
- Move the handle forward to de-loft the club
- Stand to handle and lean slightly toward the target

Putt
- Assume a normal stance and setup
- Find an intermediate target
- Smooth stroke, solid contact

Pre-swing Thoughts
- Choose the shot you're most comfortable hitting
- Trust your instinct when it comes to distance

Swing
Bump and Run
- Keep body still
- Use putting stroke (arms/shoulders)

Putt
- Lengthen backswing
- Maintain smooth acceleration
- Keep your head down

A good lag putter will never hurt himself or herself on the green. Inaccurate approach shots are nothing to the golfer who knows how to get down in two. Three-putting is just about the most frustrating failure for a good golfer. It's also the quickest route to a poor score. It's sinful (in most instances) to bogey a green hit in regulation. Not only will three-putts add strokes to your card, they'll ruin your confidence on—and off—the green.

—SKIP KENDALL

Monster Putt

MONSTER PUTTS CAN BE SCARY, especially if you lack the confidence to roll the ball to within a radius of a foot or two. According to Dave Pelz, a great short-game statistician, more than one-half of your putts will be from 30 feet or more, so there's definitely a scoring payoff for finding a way to two-putt from monster distances.

It certainly would have helped PGA Tour veteran John Cook, who faced a go-ahead, 30-foot eagle putt on the 71st hole of the 1992 British Open at Muirfield. He trailed leader Nick Faldo by one stroke when he reached the 17th hole, a 542-yard par 5, with a long-iron shot. Left with what looked like a makeable 30-footer to take the lead, Cook knocked his eagle putt two feet past the hole, and missed the tricky comeback putt for birdie. (Cook wasn't the only victim of Murfield's 17th. Twenty years earlier, Tony Jacklin three-putted the same green to fall a stroke behind eventual winner Lee Trevino.)

Anything over 30 feet is a long putt and anything over 50 feet is a monster putt. The likelihood of three-putting increases as the number of plus-30-foot putts rises.

COMMON ERRORS

One of the most common causes of poor lag putting from long distance is a faulty stroke. Many players take a short backswing and then overaccelerate the club as they come through the ball. They almost punch it. This is because the brain knew the shortened backstroke wasn't long enough to propel the ball the intended distance on the through stroke. At the last second, it said, "Pop it. Smack it. Hit it. Add more power."

Another mechanical fault that plagues players when hitting long distance putts is hitting up on the ball versus through the ball. As a player makes a longer stroke, the tendency is to allow the putter to finish too high. The ball is mis-hit—that is, struck with an ascending glancing blow. It also lofts the ball instead of sliding it along the ground before it begins rolling.

As the putting stroke gets longer it should still remain close to the ground, ensuring solid contact and constant loft after impact. One key to keeping the putter

As the putting stroke gets longer it should still remain close to the ground, ensuring solid contact and constant loft after contact.

head close to the ground on longer putts is allowing the putter head to move to the inside on the backstroke. However, at impact and through the area just before and after impact, the putter should be moving straight along the target line. Let the club come to the inside slightly on the backstroke and then down the target line through impact returning to the inside at the completion of the stroke.

STEP-BY-STEP APPROACH

Here is a step-by-step method for getting those long lag putts close enough to make the second putt.

1. Walk behind the ball and look down the line, then walk toward the hole on the side (if the putt breaks at the hole).
2. Imagine how the ball will roll in three distinct segments of the putt:
   - The initial starting line when it is traveling fastest
   - The middle segment when it rolls at a fairly constant rate of speed
   - The final third of the way when the ball slows and stops. During the third

segment, the ball will take the greatest part of the break. Visualize the path that the ball will take as it slows down and approaches the cup.

3. Envision a small circle around the cup. Aim for the cup but realize that your goal is to stop the ball somewhere in the radius of the small circle. For starters, use a radius of 21 inches, the average length of distance between the putter blade and grip, what's often recognized in informal, friendly matches as the official "gimme" distance—that which is "within the leather."

4. Make two practice strokes, visualizing the ball rolling away on the line that you've chosen to putt and then its path as it wends its way toward the hole.

5. Address the ball with your normal setup positions—make no adjustments

6. When making the stroke keep the putter close to the ground, allowing it to swing on a slight arc.

7. Keep the club moving at the same pace through the ball—do not slow down or speed up.

VERY LONG PUTT

A popular tip for very long putts is to try to get the ball inside of a three-foot circle that surrounds the hole. It sounds good, but when applied, rarely works. The best way to get a long putt close to the hole is by focusing on making the putt.

Focusing on getting the ball only inside that three-foot circle on every long putt you face accomplishes only two things: (1) It makes you sloppy, and (2) it makes you tentative. I often use the analogy of throwing darts when it comes to long putts. When throwing darts you narrow your focus on the bullseye in an effort to get as close to it as possible. If you focused on the board as a whole you would end up with a sloppy pattern of shots—and more than likely, no darts in the bullseye.

Top PGA instructor David Glenz advises similarly, "Don't lag. Focus on reading the break and rolling the ball the right speed. A putt that misses with the right speed will be a gimme. A putt you try to lay within two feet will usually leave you a three- or four-foot knee knocker."

Common Mistakes

- Taking too short a backstroke and then surging, or over accelerating, in the forward stroke
- Allowing the putter to swing too high through impact, thus striking the ball with an ascending and glancing blow

Stance and Setup

- Use a normal setup (no changes from regular stance)
- Your shoulder line, putter face, hips and toe line (if you putt with a square stance) point along lines that run parallel to your target line

Pre-stroke Thoughts

- Get behind ball and visualize path to the hole
- Focus on making the putt at the right speed to get as close as possible

Stroke

- Keep the club moving at the same pace through the ball
- When lengthening the backstroke allow the club to swing in a slight arc, staying as close to the ground as possible

I don't know anyone who likes putting downhill and left to right. Most bad misses on left-to-right stem from stroking the ball too hard and too straight. Instead, try to leave the putt short. And allow for more break than you think you see. Aiming the ball farther up the slope will help you control its speed and bring it toward the hole more softly.
—TOM WATSON

Left-to-Right Downhill Putt (for a Right-Handed Player)

ON THE 18TH HOLE of the Winged Foot Golf Club at the 1984 U.S. Open, Greg Norman had one final chance to keep his winning hopes alive in the tournament. Norman needed to hole a 45-foot downhill putt that would break left to right to force a playoff with fellow competitor Fuzzy Zoeller. With his ball sitting on the fringe, Norman opted to leave the flagstick in place. He stepped back to plan his attack.

Studying his line and estimating the pace of the putt, Norman picked out a patch of brown grass on the green as his target. This was the apex of the break. Instead of concerning himself with the hole, Norman concentrated on getting the ball to the apex with the proper speed that would then take it to the hole.

He set up in his stance, focused on his target and struck the ball perfectly. When the ball held its line through the brown grass, Norman was confident he'd holed the putt. The ball curved around and rolled down toward the cup, hit the flagstick squarely, and dropped in. (Of course, Zoeller would go on to win, but it's always better to force a playoff and lose than to never have played off at all. Or something like that.) Give Norman credit for draining a difficult putt in the most pressure-packed situation imaginable. His execution was flawless. But reaching that final destination (the hole) was only made possible by that little patch of brown grass. The key to making a left-to-right downhill putt is to focus on where the ball should start—not where you'd like it to finish.

HOLE IS THE DESTINATION, NOT THE FOCUS

A left-to-right breaking downhill putt is a very difficult shot for right-handed golfers. (The same can be said for right-to-left downhill putts for left-handed players.) The problem arises when we misdirect our concentration on the position of the hole. If the hole is your last look before striking the ball, you're going to miss more of these putts than you should.

When your last look is to the hole, your mind begins to play tricks on you. You can start to doubt and in some cases eventually abandon the line you've already calculated. The tendency is to putt more toward the hole, which leaves the ball on the short or closest side to you. You've underplayed the break.

It's very common to underplay the break. To avoid this, you must be able to locate the apex. The apex is the highest point before the ball starts to break down toward the hole. In my golf school, I ask players to judge the break on a left-to-right downhill putt and put a tee where the apex is. Invariably, the consensus calls for too little break—they usually underestimate it by at least 50 percent.

To compensate for underplaying the break, you have to hit the ball firmer. This compounds your troubles. First, it's harder for the ball to fall in the hole from the side when it's traveling faster. It will only fall if it hits dead center. In addition, if the ball misses the hole completely, you're left with a four- or five-foot putt coming back. Catching an outside edge at this speed may be even worse. The ball will spin out and sling itself six or eight feet down the hill.

The correct method is to pick the higher apex and let gravity pull the ball down the slope and fall into the hole. You've got to trust your line and putt to the apex (much like Norman did). Like most aspects of putting, the only way to improve at determining break is through practice.

DETERMINING THE BREAK

When calculating the final line, you must first survey the green. If you've played a few holes you should already have a feel for the speed of the green, so focus your attention on direction. To best calculate the slope, always begin your read from behind the ball. Examine the ground between you and the hole. Does it pitch to the

When hitting a breaking putt you must first find the "break point" or apex, the point at which the ball changes direction and begins tracking toward the hole. Stroke your ball directly at the break point and trust your judgment.

right? Left? Or is it flat? (In this case, the slope slants to the right.) To confirm your read, walk to the low side of the hole (to the right of the hole).

Once you've determined the direction of the break, you must find your apex. Trust your instinct: Your first evaluation is usually your best. That break point is your target when aligning your putt. Take your putting stroke as if that point is the hole. Once the ball gets past the apex and breaks toward the hole, you no longer control it. The slope does.

The major benefit to playing your putts with more break and less speed is you will eliminate many would-be three putts. The only thing better than tapping your second putt in after a nerve-wracking 10-footer is picking it out of the hole.

TOEING STRAIGHT DOWNHILL PUTTS

Downhill putts make most golfers uncomfortable. They're afraid of hitting the ball too firm and creating another putt that's even longer coming back. Discomfort standing over the ball can lead you to alter your mechanics from your natural putting stroke. Golfers tend to tap or jab at the ball, thus losing tempo and a degree of accuracy. You can remedy this problem by using the toe of the putter.

Hitting the ball on the toe will help "deaden" the putt. A ball hit on the toe will roll far less than a putt hit in the center with the same stroke. Instead of tapping

the ball (which is difficult to develop a feel for), you can stroke the ball, thus making a positive movement of the putter head. The ball will roll soft and true.

DOWNHILL PUTTS

Stroking downhill putts that break left to right effectively relies on good judgment. Here are a few guidelines for reference that will assist your judgment.

- **Downhill putts reduce the effective distance, because gravity carries the ball farther than if the ground were level.**
- **The greater the slope, the more the ball's roll will be affected.**
- **The faster the ball speed, the less the effect of the slope.**
- **A slope near the origination of the putt will have less effect than when the slope is near the hole.**
- **The faster the green (or shorter the grass), the more slope will affect the putt, because there's less friction against the ball.**
- **Sidehill putts tend to curl the ball farther right or left than golfers expect, often because the ball speed is slower than normal.**

LEFT-TO-RIGHT DOWNHILL PUTT (FOR A RIGHT-HANDED PLAYER)

Common Mistakes
- Looking at the hole instead of the apex
- Failing to trust your line
- Underplaying break, overplaying speed

Stance and Setup
- Align the clubface to the apex you've chosen
- Normal stance and setup

Pre-stroke Thoughts
- Let the ball fall into the hole—focus on the high side of the cup
- Focus on putting the ball to the apex; once it reaches that point, gravity will complete the job for you

Stroke
- Increase or decrease your backswing depending on the length of the putt
- Stay committed to stroking through to the apex of the putt you've chosen

When the ball dies at the hole there are four doors; the ball can go in the front, or the back, or at either side. But a ball that comes up to the hole with speed on it must hit the front door in the middle; there are no side doors, and no Sunday entrance.
—STEWART MAIDEN

Short Breaking Putt

SHORT FOUR- OR SIX-FOOT PUTTS from the sides of the hole on pitched slopes are the proverbial knee-knockers. They require precision and steady nerves. It's no time to get a case of the yips.

The most common error in making this type of putt is trying to completely take out the break. Players bang the ball into the back of the cup. It pops straight up and out or it spins around the back lip, pops out and rolls several feet away. Your four-footer for par has just turned into a seven-footer for bogey. Not good!

Before you attempt this putt determine which segment of the hole is the best entry point for the putt. With "short-breaking putts" of three to five feet, it's always some point on the high side of the hole. When the slope is severe, try to approach the hole as high as possible, allowing the ball to die into the top edge When the slope is mild, have your putt approach closer to the midpoint but still on the high side.

WATCH YOUR SPEED

Imagine the speed at which the ball should enter. Keep in mind that gravity will help balls fall into the hole if they are rolling along the edge slow enough to topple sideways on the low side (down the hill). Now imagine a speed at which you want the putt to roll and then select the break that will allow the ball to reach the hole at that speed. Plan your putt to roll no farther than 12 to 17 inches beyond the hole, should the ball not drop in.

When determining the break that will allow the ball to reach the hole at the speed you've imagined, do some quick surveying first. Back off, walk below the hole toward the front of the green and look at the ball, hole, and slope. This longer view from the low side will give you a better understanding of the overall pitch of the slope, and its degree of severity. It will confirm the direction the putt will break and help you calculate how much break it will take.

Now, from behind your ball, select the apex (a.k.a. the break point). The apex is also that spot where the slope begins to control the speed and direction of the putt. With the break point identified, you can now plan the starting line of your putt. Given the proper speed, you will be able to roll the ball along your chosen starting line, over the break point, and let the pitch of the slope take the ball down to the hole.

First imagine the speed at which you want the putt to roll and then select the break that will allow the ball to reach the hole at that speed. Plan your putt to roll no farther than 12 to 17 inches beyond the hole.

A drill to improve your skill on breaking putts is to cover the low side of the hole with a card. This will help you narrow your focus on the high side of the hole, which is where you want the ball to enter.

THE ELUSIVE BREAK POINT

One method to finding the break point is "seeing the line." Crouch behind the ball, select a break point, and—in your mind's eye—set the ball in motion. Watch the ball reach the break point and angle back toward the cup. This sounds rather simple, but don't underestimate the power of imagination. Great putters have great visualization—they see the putts going in the hole.

After you've chosen the break point, move to the side of the ball and take two practice strokes. Match the length of your backstroke with the length of the forward stroke that will propel the ball to the break point.

Align the putter head to the break point. Set up hips and shoulders parallel to the target line, eyes over the ball, arms under the shoulders. Breathe deeply, slowly exhaling just before you stroke the ball. Take one final look at the break point, your target, bring your eyes back to the ball, and stroke the putt. After that, all you can do is listen for that sweet sound of the golf ball finding its mark.

Don't make the mistake of focusing on the hole when hitting these short-breaking putts. Your last look should be on an intermediate target along the putt's starting line. In the case of short putts, the intermediate target should be the break point.

DRILLS

Here are two drills to help you on short-sloping putts.

1. Third of the Hole

First, find a good uphill putt on the practice or putting green. Cover the low side of the hole with a scorecard (you can secure the card to the ground with a couple of tees). The idea is that sidehill putts need to hit the top side of the hole. If you putt your ball so that it enters the hole too low, it will roll over the card and not fall into the hole. That's the same as a miss. This will help you narrow your focus on the high side of the hole, which is where you want all of your breaking putts to approach the hole.

2. Through the Gate

Another drill to improve your stroke on breaking putts is "Through the Gate." Find a curving, right-to-left or left-to-right breaking putt on the practice putting green. Place two tees roughly two inches away from each other at a 45-degree angle one inch from the high side of the hole. The objective is to hole the putt through the gate. If you play too little break, or over-power the break with a forceful stroke, the ball will strike the front tee and rebound away from the cup. Only the most accurately struck putt and a perfect read will allow the ball to pass through the gate and into the hole.

Common Mistakes
- Trying to eliminate the break by ramming the putt into the back of the cup
- Focusing on the hole instead of the break point or apex point of the putt

Stance and Setup
- Align the putter head to the intermediate target, the break point
- Set hips and shoulders parallel to target line, eyes over ball, arms under shoulders

Pre-stroke Thoughts
- Match backstroke with length of forward stroke needed to propel ball to break point
- Visualize ball toppling into hole from top side of hole
- Remind yourself, "Maintain a light grip pressure and make a smooth stroke"

Stroke
- Breathe deeply, slowly before stroke
- Take final look at break point (target)
- Bring eyes back to ball and stroke the ball

Index

About the Authors

Todd Sones, who began his career as golf professional in 1981, has been recognized as one of the Top 100 Teachers in America by *Golf Magazine* for the past decade and has been selected twice as PGA Teacher of the Year in Illinois. Among his students are several PGA and LPGA tour players, including Robert Gamez, Scott McCarron, Paul Goydos, Steve Jones, Jay Williamson, Stephanie Louden and Hilary Lunke, 2003 U.S. Women's Open Champion.

Sones operates the IMPACT GOLF SCHOOL, one of the Top 25 Golf Schools in America, in Vernon Hills, Illinois, and THE SCORING ZONE, a short-game school at the PGA Tour Academy, World Golf Village in St. Augustine, Florida. He is the author of *Lights-Out Putting: A Mind, Body, and Soul Approach to Golf's Game Within the Game* and has written more than 50 golf instruction articles for *Golf Magazine* and *Golf Tips*, and has appeared numerous times on The Golf Channel's *Academy Live* show.

Todd Sones can be reached at:

> Impact Golf School
> Whitedeer Run Golf Club
> 250 West Greggs Parkway
> Vernon Hills, IL 60061
> Phone: 847-549-8673
> www.Toddsones.com

John Monteleone has edited, written and/or collaborated on several golf books, including *Lowdown from the Lesson Tee: Correcting 40 of Golf's Most Misunderstood Teaching Tips* by David Glenz, 1998 National PGA Teacher of the Year, and *The Little Book of Putting* by T. J. Tomasi, Ph.D. He is the editorial director and manager of Mountain Lion, Inc., a book development company and literary agency specializing in sports, reference, health, how-to, fitness, business and professional subjects.